World War I

The
MILITARY HISTORY
of the
UNITED STATES

Christopher Chant

WORLD WAR I

MARSHALL CAVENDISH
NEW YORK · LONDON · TORONTO · SYDNEY

Library Edition Published 1992

© Marshall Cavendish Limited 1992

Published by
Marshall Cavendish Corporation
2415 Jerusalem Avenue
PO Box 587
North Bellmore
New York 11710

Series created by Graham Beehag Book Design

Series Editor	Maggi McCormick
Consultant Editors	James R. Arnold
	Roberta Wiener
Sub Editor	Julie Cairns
Designer	Graham Beehag
Illustrators	John Batchelor
	Steve Lucas
	Terry Forest
	Colette Brownrigg
Indexer	Mark Dartford

The publishers wish to thank the following organizations who have supplied photographs:

The National Archives, Washington. United States Navy, United States Marines, United States Army, United States Air Force, Department of Defense, Library of Congress, The Smithsonian Institution.

The publishers gratefully thank the U.S. Army Military History Institute, Carlisle Barracks, PA. for the use of archive material for the following witness accounts:

Page 66
From Tom Carroll's Diary in the papers of Ira Redlinger, 1st Infantry Brigade, 16th Infantry; in World War I.

Page 129
From the letters and Diary of Bugler Howard Webster Munder, Company G, 109th Infantry; in World War I, 28th Division.

Library of Congress Cataloging-in-Publication Data

Chant, Christopher.
    The Military History of the United States / Christopher Chant –
Library ed.
        p. cm.
    Includes bibliographical references and index.
    Summary: Surveys the wars that have directly influenced the
    United States., from the Revolutionary War through the Cold War.
    ISBN 1-85435-359-4 ISBN 1-85435-361-9 (set)
    1. United States - History, Military - Juvenile literature.
|1. United States - History, Military.| I. Title.
t181.C52 1991
973 - dc20   90 - 19547
                                                          CIP
                                                           AC

Printed in Singapore by Times Offset PTE Ltd
Bound in the United States

Contents

As the two major European power blocs lurched toward war in 1914, the United States found itself with the world's third largest navy. But its army was tiny by European standards, with a strength of 100,000 men authorized by Congress in 1902. The army was also poorly equipped by European standards, especially in heavy weapons. Furthermore, the army was divided over the reforms instigated by Secretary of War Elihu Root between 1901 and 1903. There was a power struggle between the comparatively new General Staff and the heads of the War Department's long-established bureaux. In addition, throughout the army's officer corps there was still heated debate about the recommendation of Colonel Emory Upton that the traditional militia system should be abandoned in favor of the concept of an expandable regular army.

The event that sparked the European tinderbox occurred on June 28, 1914. The heir to the Austro-Hungarian throne, Achduke Franz Ferdinand, was assassinated by a fanatical Serbian nationalist at Sarajevo, in the Austro-Hungarian province of Bosnia. The balance of European power between the Triple Alliance (Germany, Austria-Hungary, and Italy) and the Triple Entente (France, Russia, and the United Kingdom) was then capsized by the series of threats and counterthreats that followed.

Serbia met only part of an Austro-Hungarian ultimatum, and with German backing, Austria-Hungary declared war against Serbia on July 28. To support Serbia, Russia ordered mobilization against Austria-Hungary, whereupon Germany declared war against Russia on August 1. In accordance with a long-standing plan, Germany also declared war against France on August 3 and began an invasion through neutral Bel-

The event that sparked off World War I was the assassination of Archduke Franz Ferdinand, the heir to the throne of Austria-Hungary, and his wife, who are seen here only hours before their deaths. Franz Ferdinand is on the left.

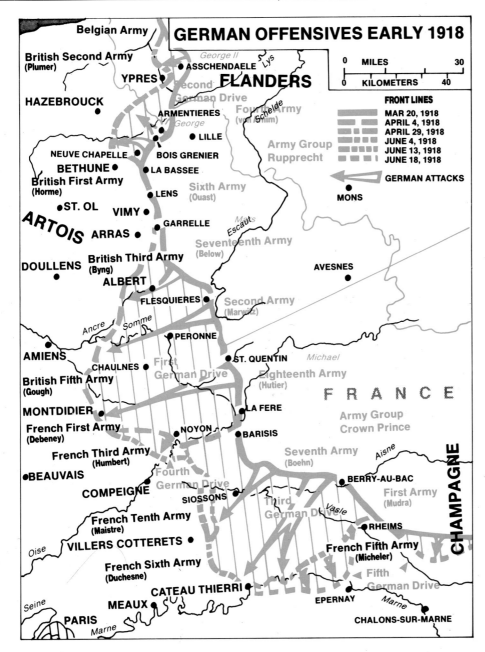

GERMAN OFFENSIVES EARLY 1918

Belgian Army

British Second Army (Plumer)

ASSCHENDAELE

YPRES

FLANDERS

HAZEBROUCK

Second German Drive

Fourth Army (von Arnim)

ARMENTIERES

LILLE

NEUVE CHAPELLE

BOIS GRENIER

Army Group Rupprecht

BETHUNE

LA BASSEE

British First Army (Horme)

LENS

Sixth Army (Ouast)

MONS

ST. OL

VIMY

GARRELLE

ARTOIS

ARRAS

Seventeenth Army (Below)

DOULLENS

British Third Army (Byng)

AVESNES

ALBERT

FLESQUIERES

Second Army (Marwitz)

Ancre

Somme

PERONNE

AMIENS

CHAULNES

First German Drive

ST. QUENTIN

Michael

Eighteenth Army (Hutier)

British Fifth Army (Gough)

FRANCE

MONTDIDIER

LA FERE

Army Group Crown Prince

French First Army (Debeney)

NOYON

BARISIS

French Third Army (Humbert)

Seventh Army (Boehn)

Aisne

BEAUVAIS

Fourth German Drive

BERRY-AU-BAC

COMPEIGNE

SIOSSONS

Third German Drive

First Army (Mudra)

French Tenth Army (Maistre)

Vasle

CHAMPAGNE

Oise

VILLERS COTTERETS

RHEIMS

French Sixth Army (Duchesne)

French Fifth Army (Micheler)

Fifth German Drive

CATEAU THIERRI

Seine

MEAUX

EPERNAY

Marne

PARIS

Marne

CHALONS-SUR-MARNE

Scale:
0 — MILES — 30
0 — KILOMETERS — 40

FRONT LINES

MAR 20, 1918
APRIL 4, 1918
APRIL 29, 1918
JUNE 4, 1918
JUNE 13, 1918
JUNE 18, 1918

GERMAN ATTACKS

Map of the main German offensives during early 1918.

gium and Luxembourg. The United Kingdom declared war against Germany on August 4 because of the invasion of Belgium, and the initial confrontation was completed by Austria-Hungary's declaration of war against Russia on August 6.

Germany and Austria-Hungary were soon known as the Central Powers, and were later joined by Turkey (the vast but crumbling Ottoman Empire) and Bulgaria. France, Russia, the United Kingdom, and Belgium became known as the Allied Powers and were later joined by Italy and Rumania. Italy was treaty-bound to join Austria-Hungary and Germany, but at first declared herself neutral on the grounds that the war had been caused by Austria-Hungary.

Other countries were later drawn into the conflict by a variety of ambitions, but the United States declared her neutrality on August 4, 1914.

Main Theaters: the Eastern and Western Fronts

Except for the small yet bitter war

A recruiting poster for the Corps of Engineers.

between Austria-Hungary and Serbia in the northwestern Balkans, the two main theaters of war were those between the Central Powers and Russia (generally known as the Eastern Front) and between Germany and the western Allies in Belgium and France (generally known as the Western Front). Other fronts were later opened in Italy, the northern Balkans, the Dardanelles, the Caucasus, Palestine, and Mesopotamia, but none of them approached the Eastern and Western Fronts in sheer size and strategic importance.

The wars on both of these fronts started as campaigns of great movement, but soon settled into savage operations of infrequent movement on the Eastern Front, and virtually no movement at all on the Western Front. Men and equipment were fed into these vicious meat-grinders in ever larger numbers and quantities, but the destruction of men and materiel that followed did not achieve any significant breakthrough that might have led to victory for either side.

The front on which the main

protagonists expected ultimate victory to come was the Western Front. Here the Germans faced the Belgians, British, and French in an evermore complex series of trench lines protected by barbed wire and machine guns. The generals were so short of tactical and strategic ideas that they could conceive of only one tactic: a pounding of the enemy's lines by huge artillery barrages, and then an infantry attack intended to break through the enemy's trenches and so open the way for the cavalry to sweep into the enemy's rear areas. Here, it was thought, they could wreak the type of destruction that would cause the enemy to crumble and allow more attacking troops to break through.

The Grim Nature of Trench Warfare

However, the artillery never managed to destroy all the barbed wire or more than a small proportion of the enemy's front-line bunkers and machine gun nests. The lift-

A telling image of World War I: sitting in a splinter-proof shelter, an American artilleryman writes home.

ing of an artillery barrage meant that an infantry attack was about to arrive, so the defenders would emerge from their deep, shell-proof bunkers to man the rifle positions and machine gun nests. From there, they could scythe down the infantry, which was advancing slowly through the devastation of No Man's Land toward barbed wire entanglements that the artillery never seemed to be able to touch. Even when the attackers reached and seized the enemy's front-line trenches, their casualties were always so high that a breakthrough was impossible, and a successful defense against the inevitable counterattack was difficult.

Such conditions were general on the Western Front by November 1914, and the memory of 1915 and 1916 remains scarred by names such as Ypres, Verdun, and Somme among a host of Belgian and French places that have come to mean the useless sacrifice of millions of lives for no real gain.

While this deadlocked land war dragged on, Germany and the United Kingdom were involved in a naval war designed to yield the same type of strategic result. The British used the battleships, battle-cruisers, and cruisers of their mighty navy to blockade Germany, cutting all German maritime trade and preventing German warships from bursting out into the Atlantic to harry Allied merchant shipping. Although little appreciated, this blockade did have an enormous impact on Germany, for so badly affected were her supplies of oil, raw materials, and food that the country was on the verge of collapse by 1918.

The Start of U-boat Warfare

Germany tried to exert the same pressures on the western Allies. The United

The *Lusitania*
For further references see pages
11, 12

The squalid and crowded conditions in the trenches is shown in this picture of Russian infantrymen waiting to go over the top.

Kingdom was most reliant on shipping for all her essential supplies and therefore possessed the largest and potentially most vulnerable merchant marine fleet. In the war against British shipping, the major German weapon was the U-boat (submarine). When the U-boat campaign started in 1915, Germany had only 27 such boats, but they were soon sinking more than 150,000 tons of merchant shipping each month.

The captains of these boats could not always identify their intended targets with complete accuracy, and it was inevitable, therefore, that some neutral ships were attacked. The first American victim was the tanker S.S. *Gulflight*, which was torpedoed and sunk on May 1, 1915, with the loss of two lives. This event caused great consternation in the United States, but far worse was to come within the week.

The Sinking of the *Lusitania*

On May 7, 1915, the British luxury liner *Lusitania* was torpedoed without warning by the U-20 in Irish waters. Before the ship sailed from New York, the German embassy in Washington had warned Americans not to sail on her, but among the 1,198 people who lost their lives were 124 Americans. The American public was deeply shocked, and a strong American diplomatic protest was lodged with the Germans. Up to this time, most Americans had been unable to come to

any real understanding of President Woodrow Wilson's demand for impartiality of thought about World War I, and had also displayed no real interest in an active involvement in the war. There had certainly been American indignation about the German submarine campaign, but there had also been American resentment about a comparable British campaign of surface blockade that affected American shipping and was considered just as reprehensible as the German submarine campaign.

With the sinking of the *Lusitania* and the loss of many American lives, this feeling began to change. Membership of patriotic bodies began to increase, and more attention was paid to men who had suggested a higher level of American military preparation.

Among these were the voices of men such as ex-President Theodore Roosevelt, two ex-secretaries of war, Elihu Root and Henry L. Stimson, and a recent chief of staff, Major General Leonard Wood, who had retired just over a year after the inauguration of Wilson's peace-favoring administration. Yet though greater heed was slowly paid to the warnings of such men, this was only in the east. Southerners and westerners paid little attention to the war, while in the Midwest a concentration of German Americans began to develop a strong isolationist voice. There was also a tide of pacifist feeling, whose most influential adherent was Secretary of State William Jennings Bryan. Bryan agreed with the presi-

U-boats
For further references see pages
12, 13, 15, 16, *17*, 18, 19, *20*, 116, *117*

Woodrow Wilson
For further references see pages
12, *13*, 14, 15, 16, 17, 22, 35, 102, 114, 116, *122*, 127, *128*

Washington D.C.
For further references see pages
14, 15, 20, 35, 114, 116, 124

One of the last pictures taken of the *Lusitania*. The sinking of this ship outraged public opinion in the U.S.

Left: Commanding the ill-fated *Lusitania* on her last voyage was Captain Turner.

Below: The body of a dead American passenger from the *Lusitania* is brought ashore under the "Stars and Stripes" at Queenstown in Ireland. Pictures such as this helped to inflame American anger against Germany.

Bottom: Dubbed "wolves of the sea," submarines such as these two German U-boats very nearly brought the United Kingdom to her knees, but their activities eventually brought the United States into World War I on the side of the United Kingdom, France, and their allies.

dent that the sinking of the *Lusitania* demanded a strong American protest. Wilson was dissatisfied with the German answer, and sent a second, stronger note to the Germans, insisting on the right of neutrals to trade by sea without hindrance. Bryan disagreed with the second note and resigned.

End of the First U-boat Campaign

The German submarine campaign continued through the summer of 1915 to the accompaniment of notes from Wilson. Then on August 19, 1915, the British liner *Arabic* was sunk, and the deaths of another four Americans produced such a wave of diplomatic and popular anger that Germany announced a change in policy during September. The U-boats would now sink passenger liners only after issuing a warning that would allow the potential target to stop and implement safety measures. It became clear after the war, however, that this move was an astute way of gaining an easy propaganda victory at a time when

Germany's U-boat fleet had been reduced to very small numbers.

All the while, American trade with Europe continued. This trade served the Allies more than the Germans, for British ships proved adept in halting and holding American ships loaded with food for the Central Powers just long enough for the food to rot. In mid-1915, the British added cotton to the list of contraband that would be seized and instituted a blacklist of American firms trading with the Central Powers. The southern states were particularly hard-hit by this move, but the munitions trade with the Allies had by now become so profitable that few others were worried. In October 1915, Wilson repealed an earlier prohibition of loans to the fighting powers, which stimulated the munitions trade even more.

By the beginning of 1916, the overall feeling in the United States was still against any American involvement in the war. However, there was a gradual shift in sympathy toward the Allies, whose excellent propaganda campaign was aided by the discovery of clumsy efforts by German military attaches in the United States to organize spying and sabotage. The episode that most annoyed Americans with the Germans' high-handed approach was the arrival of a U-boat that surfaced in Newport Harbor, sent an officer ashore to deliver a letter to the German ambassador, and then submerged to sink nine Allied merchant ships off the coast of New England.

Wilson was still convinced of the need

A man devoted to peace, President Woodrow Wilson was compelled to take the United States into its first major intercontinental war.

for the United States to remain neutral, and he sought to persuade the fighting powers of the need to establish international rules of submarine warfare. Yet the president was also aware of the drift of events. In February 1916, he demanded that the U.S. Navy should become "the greatest navy in the world." At the same time, he suggested a wide program of military training for civilians in case the United States was soon faced with the problem of "putting raw levies of inexperienced men onto the modern field of battle."

Deteriorating Relations with Germany

American relations with Germany continued to worsen. On February 21, 1916, Germany announced that, from March 1, armed merchant ships would be treated as warships, and on March 24, the French ship *Sussex* was sunk with the loss of several American lives. It was suggested to Wilson by Colonel Edward M. House, his personal adviser, and by Secretary of State Robert Lansing, that relations with Germany should now be broken off. Wilson decided instead on an ultimatum, couched in the form of a diplomatic note, that the United States would sever diplomatic relations unless Germany agreed to leave passenger and merchant ships unhindered.

On May 10, Germany issued the so-called "Sussex pledge" stating that passenger ships would not be sunk without warning, and ending the extended U-boat campaign that had been launched in February. Germany also questioned why the United States was being harder with Germany than the United Kingdom, and Wilson saw that unless he could balance the American approach to the naval efforts of these two major protagonists, the German pledge of limited U-boat warfare would be short-lived. Wilson's protest about the British blockade achieved nothing, and the president's offer to negotiate a peace settlement achieved precisely the same result.

Throughout the period, Wilson's open support of neutrality was balanced by a

Pancho Villa's continued "revolutionary" activities in northern Mexico, accompanied by the threat of more raids into the United States, meant that sizeable American forces had to be kept in Texas, New Mexico, and Arizona. It was only on July 27, 1920, that Villa finally surrendered at the end of the renewed civil war that had broken out in April of that year.

steadily growing but less obvious support for military preparation. This resulted from the president's own assessment of the situation, and also from the urgings of Secretary of War Lindley M. Garrison. In September 1915, Garrison added to his annual report, prepared by the General Staff, a section titled "A Proper Military Policy for the United States." This document marked the effective end of Upton's notion of an expandable army. What was now suggested was a development of the traditional American policy of a citizen army: the regular army would be more than doubled, the National Guard would receive additional federal support, and a 400,000-man volunteer force would be raised. This last was to be called the Continental Army and would be a trained reserve under federal control, while the National Guard would remain under state control.

Wilson refused to consider anything but a small increase in the strength of the regular army, but was attracted by the idea of the Continental Army. In Congress, the idea of the Continental Army drew Senate support, but foundered on the objections of the House of Representatives, where many congressmen felt the idea was designed to undermine the National Guard. As a counter, the objecting congressmen prepared a bill demanding greater federal support for the National Guard, the acceptance of federal standards by the National Guard, and agreement by the National Guard to respond to any presidential call to service. Wilson switched his support to this bill and so added to the issues that prompted Garrison's resignation.

At this point, trouble with Pancho Villa flared on the border with Mexico. The demand for a larger active strength proved decisive. It was finally decided that a citizen army should indeed be the core of American military strength, but that this citizen army should be the National Guard rather than a Continental Army.

The National Defense Act of 1916

The bill was passed in May 1916 and became the National Defense Act in June. The act angered backers of the concept of an expandable army, but it did produce a better U.S. Army. However, it was still not comparable in any way in size and capabilities with those armies that were now standard in Europe. The act also placed severe limitations on the General Staff by limiting the number of officers who could serve at any one time on the General Staff in or around Washington.

The main provision of the National Defense Act was to increase the authorized peacetime strength of the army to 175,000 men over a period of five years, and its wartime strength to nearly 300,000 men. At the same time, federal funding was to be combined with federal standards of organization and training to create an effective National Guard, which was to be more than quadrupled in size to 400,000 men and obliged to respond to a presidential command. The act also provided for an Officers' Reserve Corps and Enlisted Reserve Corps, and in wartime only, for a Volunteer Army, later called the National Army. The nucleus of an expanded officer corps was to be created by a Reserve Officers' Training Corps program at colleges and universities.

Just as important, the National Defense Act gave the president great powers to place orders for defense materiel, and to compel industry to comply with these orders. The act also required the secretary of war to undertake a survey of all the country's arms and munitions industries. Only a few months later, Congress showed that its concern with the United States' military capability was not a passing political phase by creating a Council of National Defense. The task of the council, which was made up of industry and labor leaders supported by an advisory commission of the secretaries of the main government departments, was a study of economic mobilization. Another step toward preparing the United States more thoroughly for war was the creation of the U.S. Shipping Board, whose task was to regulate sea transport while also developing a naval auxiliary fleet and a merchant marine.

Stalemate on the Western Front

By the beginning of 1917, Germany's leaders had come to the conclusion that their manpower losses in the Battles of Verdun and the Somme had been so catastrophic that Germany would have to go onto the defensive on the Western Front. The German leaders were also fully aware that only offensive action of some type could win the war. They therefore decided to readopt a policy of unrestricted warfare by the U-boat arm, which now had nearly 200 boats. The overall plan for the campaign was an attack against all shipping in British and French waters, regardless of nationality, with the intention of ending the war within six months. It was a calculated gamble by

the Germans, who realized that the offensive could bring the United States into the war on the Allied side. However, they believed that they could starve France and the United Kingdom into surrender before the United States could raise, train, and ship substantial forces across the Atlantic.

The German embassy in Washington tried to buy additional time by urging Wilson to continue his effort to find a peaceful solution to the war. On January 31, 1917, the German leadership announced that a policy of unrestricted U-boat warfare would be implemented from the following day, and that any vessel, Allied or neutral, was subject to attack without warning.

Wilson hoped that he could still find an alternative to war and, as the rest of the world waited to see the American

A patriotic display by the men of the 164th Depot Brigade at Fort Funston, Kansas. The creation of depots and other bases was the first priority of the U.S. Army as war approached, since they provided for the men of the vastly expanding army to be housed, clothed, fed, and trained for deployment to Europe.

reaction, the president went to Congress on February 3. What the president wanted was not a declaration of war, but the breaking of diplomatic relations. Wilson hoped that his major step, only one remove from war, would finally persuade Germany of the United States' grave concern and force her to call off the unrestricted U-boat campaign.

The "Zimmermann Telegram"

What Wilson did not yet know was that the British had in the previous month intercepted a coded telegram from the German foreign minister, Arthur Zimmermann, to his ambassador in Mexico. Sent on January 19, the telegram contained the suggestion that in the event of war between Germany and the United States, Germany would conclude an alliance with Mexico which, the Germans

additionally hoped, would also persuade Japan to enter the alliance. In return, Germany offered financial and technical support for the reconquest of the former Mexican territories of Arizona, New Mexico, and Texas.

British naval intelligence decoded the telegram, but delayed its release until it could provide the Americans with proof of its authenticity without allowing the Germans to know that their diplomatic code had been broken. On February 23, a copy was handed over to Walter Hines Page, the American ambassador in the United Kingdom, who immediately forwarded it to the State Department. Wilson was immediately told of the telegram by the State Department, but still held back from urging an American declaration of war.

After considerable debate in the highest circles, Wilson authorized the release of the telegram's contents to the press on March 1. The president's

African-American troops were used mainly for rear-area service tasks in France. The laughter on the face of this private during a practice drill does not mean that gas-mask practice was less important.

President Wilson delivers his war message to Congress, signaling the entry of the United States into World War I.

intention was not to inflame the American public toward a declaration of war, but raise enough anger that public pressure would urge Congress to agree with Wilson's next move. This step was the intention to arm American merchant ships, most of which were lying idle in port because of the U-boat threat. The president hoped that this would strengthen the message already relayed by the breaking of diplomatic relations, and so help persuade the Germans to call off the U-boat campaign.

Wilson clearly did not anticipate the wave of indignant anti-German fury that swept through Congress and most of the American public. The only other voices heard were those of pacifist and pro-German organizations, who denounced the Zimmermann telegram as an obvious British "plant." American intelligence sources were sure about its authenticity, however, and Zimmermann himself soon confirmed the fact, neatly cutting the ground from under the pacifists and pro-Germans.

The American Declaration of War

On March 13, the State and Navy Departments announced that all American mer-

A poster urges greater effort on what was later called the ''home front.''

through 54 divisions of the French army and made it completely unable to undertake any real military operations. These events occurred at about the same time as the American declaration of war, and were followed by other disasters before the Americans could mobilize their potential.

First, the British attempted to take the pressure off the French in June with the modestly successful Battle of Messines, which provided the strategic and tactical elbow room for the 3rd Battle of Ypres. Launched on the last day of July 1917, this ghastly slogging match achieved virtually nothing except the further bleeding of exhausted armies. Indeed, it is now generally known by the name of its last phase, the Battle of Passchendaele, a word that has passed into the English vocabulary as a synonym for senseless, hopeless slaughter.

Second, after failing to make progress in northeastern Italy during the 10th and 11th Battles of the Isonzo, the Italians were by the end of October at the receiving end of an offensive launched by the Austro-Hungarians with German assistance. This 12th Battle of the Isonzo turned into an Italian rout known as the Battle of Caporetto, which cost Italy 40,000 men killed and 275,000 taken prisoner. The Central Powers suffered only 20,000 losses, and they captured vast quantities of materiel, including more than 2,000 guns. The Allies had to stabilize the position on the Italian front by sending in 11 British and French divisions that could not really be spared from the Western Front.

chant ships passing through the war zone would be fitted with defensive armament. Even so, four more American ships were sunk in the next few weeks, resulting in the deaths of another 15 Americans. Wilson finally had to face the need to reflect public opinion, as well as the failure of his efforts to secure peace. He therefore went to Congress on April 2 and asked for a declaration of war. On April 6, 1917, the United States declared war on Germany. A declaration of war on Austria-Hungary did not follow until December 7, 1917.

The American declaration came at the time of the Allies' lowest point in World War I. In March, Russia had been racked by revolution, thereby jeopardizing continued Russian operations on the Eastern Front. On the Western Front, the disastrous Franco-British offensive of April resulted in more catastrophic losses, followed by a widespread mutiny that swept

Crisis at Sea

The succession of crises on land was more than balanced in the middle part of the year by Allied problems at sea. The first full month of the Germans' unrestricted U-boat campaign had resulted in the loss of 781,000 tons of Allied and neutral shipping. Given such losses, the Royal Navy calculated that the United Kingdom would run out of food and other essential raw materials by the end of July, raising the possibility that the United Kingdom would have to sue for peace in October.

The U.S. Navy Gets Into the War

Conditions did not reach this point. From May 10, a convoy system was adopted. Already urged by Admiral Sir David Beatty with the support of an American officer, Rear Admiral William S. Sims, the policy was forced on a reluctant Royal Navy by Prime Minister David Lloyd George, and it proved an immediate success. The U-boats were now denied unprotected random targets dotted all over the Atlantic. Instead, they had to make their attacks on convoys whose close grouping made them more difficult to find and more dangerous to attack when they were detected, since they had warship escorts.

These and other crises finally persuaded the Allies that overall conduct of the war demanded unity of command. The Conference of Rapallo was held on November 5, 1917, to try to thrash out an inter-Allied agreement, but was only partially successful. None of the Allies was prepared to see its forces under foreign command, but it was decided to create a Supreme War Council with political and military representatives from all the Allied powers. Though this action fell short of what the situation really demanded, it was nevertheless a step in the right direction.

While these problems were unfolding in Europe and the Atlantic, there was little that the United States could do in the way of short-term assistance to the Allied cause. Despite the National Defense Act of 1916, the United States was still far from ready for war, but the Navy could begin to make its contribution. American destroyers began to take part in the convoy escort forces. From early May, six American destroyers were involved in the task, and by the end of the summer, 37 American destroyers were active on the Atlantic runs. Further reinforcement of the Allied cause came in December 1917 with the arrival of four American dreadnought battleships. Forming the 6th Battle Squadron of the Royal Navy's grand fleet, they were coal-fired ships specifically requested by the British to replace five obsolete British pre-dreadnought battleships that had been paid off so that their crews could be redeployed to cruisers, destroyers, and submarines.

The success of the convoy system may be judged from the fact that losses to the U-boats declined during the second

The movement of the American Expeditionary Force's men and equipment from the United States to France was a huge logistical operation that lasted from mid-1917 right through to the end of World War I. This is a convoy bound for France in October 1918.

A large part of the burden in the campaign against U-boats operating in the Atlantic was borne by the U.S. Navy. One of the service's most important assets in this task was the large number of destroyers available. They included the flush-decked destroyers of the "Wickes" class, and this photograph shows a 1918 drill for the crew of an unprotected 4-inch gun on one of them, the U.S.S. *Little*, which carried four such weapons as her primary gun armament.

half of the year. The December loss was less than 400,000 tons, and although the year's figure was more than 8,000,000 tons, new construction offset this total, with the full weight of the large American shipbuilding industry yet to make itself felt.

The U.S. Army could not get into action nearly as quickly. Including those parts of the National Guard serving along the Mexican border under federal command, the army numbered only 210,000 men, with another 97,000 National Guardsmen still under state command. The Allies had found that the smallest practical maneuver formation for Western Front operations was the division, a combined-arms force mustering up to 12,000 men, but as yet, there was no single American division. At its headquarters in Washington, the General Staff had just 19 officers because of the restrictions placed on it by the National Defense Act. The army had gained some operational experience in Mexico during 1916, but the main effect of these operations had been to highlight operational limitations and

equipment shortages in everything but the Springfield Model 1903 rifle, of which there were about 890,000 available.

Given the army's lack of strength and the United States' entry into the war on the issue of unrestricted U-boat warfare, it could have been argued that the United States should restrict its contribution to the naval war. But this view was never actively considered by the American public or the administration. Indeed, as early as the president's war message to Congress, it was clear that American soldiers were to be sent to Europe as part of a major effort to defeat Germany and so end the war directly.

The president, Congress, and the government all moved with considerable speed to implement the necessary war effort. The president established the Emergency Fleet Corporation to increase and control the merchant marine, on which the movement of an army to Europe and then its supply would depend. Congress authorized a $7,000,000,000 bond issue, and the Treasury Department started a $2,000,000,000 "Liberty Loan."

The First American Division

At the same time, the General Staff decided that at least one division should be created and moved as rapidly as possible to France as confirmation of the United States' real intent to participate in the land battle. The 1st Division was created on the basis of four regular infantry regiments recalled from the Mexican border and brought up to strength by recruits as well as men from other regiments. The divisional staff was formed around a nucleus of regular officers boosted by Reserve officers.

By mid-June 1916, the 1st Division was embarking in New York, and the scenes of dockside confusion were not unlike those at Tampa during the Spanish-American War in 1898. It also became clear that a shortage of weapons was not the only problem: some men had not even heard of the weapons they were supposed to receive and had therefore not had even theoretical training in how to use them. Yet the division was finally despatched to France as the precursor of the American Expeditionary Force, and on July 4, 1917, a battalion of the 16th Infantry Regiment marched through Paris to be greeted by wild French enthusiasm.

This could not disguise the fact, however, that the 1st Division needed many months of intensive training before it was ready to move into even a quiet sector of the Western Front.

Pershing Commands in France

Command of the A.E.F. was entrusted by the president to Major General John J. Pershing, who was junior to five other major generals, but whose performance

Men of the 7th Infantry Regiment bid farewell to their loved ones before embarking for France, in New York during 1917. This was the first time the vast majority of the American soldiers had ever left the country.

Liberty Bonds were the war loan bonds of World War I. The Liberty Loan Act was passed by Congress on April 24, 1917, and authorized the Treasury to issue a public subscription for $2 billion in bonds designed to pay for American participation in World War I. The subscription for these 3·5 percent convertible gold bonds was handled by Secretary of the Treasury McAdoo.

as head of the Mexican Punitive Expedition in the previous year had impressed Wilson. Less than three weeks after his appointment, Pershing left for France with the mission of surveying the military situation there in order to provide the War Department with an estimate of the forces he would need. Pershing soon reported that he would need a million men by the end of 1918, with provision for 3,000,000 later. It had already become clear that the A.E.F. would need forces far larger

than those likely to be provided by the regular and volunteer forces, so on May 19, 1917, Congress had created a draft system by passing the Selective Service Act. The nature and operation of the draft system in the Civil War was studied carefully before the creation of the Selective Service Bill, and the resulting act was a model of its type. It eliminated such unfair practices as bounties, substitutes, and bought exemptions, and made sure that conscripts served for the duration of

Sergeant, Infantry, U.S. Army, France, 1917

This sergeant is typical of the "doughboys" who first arrived in France at St. Nazaire during June 1917. As a result of its experience in the Spanish-American War of 1898, the U.S. Army had adopted a well-designed and well-made olive drab (khaki) uniform in 1902, and the equipment was made of canvas duck and cotton webbing pioneered by Captain Anson Mills in his experiments 30 years earlier. From head to toe, the uniform of this sergeant includes the M1912 campaign hat in khaki brown rabbitskin felt (with its crown shaped in the "Montana" style, four ventilation eyelets, an interior sweatband of leather, a leather chinstrap, and cords in arm-of-service colors), the M1912 khaki tunic (with a standing collar, four patch pockets, five front and four pocket buttons, and dull bronze collar disks with "US" on the right and branch-of-service emblem on the left), the M1912 semi-breeches, the M1910 canvas leggings laced through eyelets at the front, and M1904 "marching shoes" in russet brown leather with the flesh-side in and the rough-side out. The equipment included the M1910 rifle belt with ten pouches each holding two five-round clips, the M1910 first aid pouch, the M1910 water canteen with its cup in a fabric carrier, the M1910 haversack (washing kit, rations, and mess tin) and pack carrier (clothing changes, blankets, groundsheet/poncho, tent cloth, and accessories), the M1903/05 Springfield rifle, M1905 bayonet, and M1910 shovel.

Above: The effort to get large numbers of American troops into battle on the Western Front was enormous. This photograph shows part of a setting-up exercise that involved 10,000 men on an American base during 1918.

Opposite Above: This is the band of the Great Lakes Naval Training School parading in Cleveland, Ohio, on April 6, 1918, the first anniversary of the United States' declaration of war on Germany.

Opposite Below: American field artillerymen parade with their horsedrawn light guns.

the war. It was felt that the army might suffer in public esteem if it operated the draft system itself, so this task was allocated to local civilian boards. They were permitted to grant exemptions to men filling essential jobs or having particular family obligations, but were required to guarantee the registration of all men between the ages of 21 and 30, an age bracket later extended to 18 and 45.

Enter the Draft

The Selective Service Act fixed the basic shape of an army that was planned as an expansion of three basic organizations. The core of the service was the regular army, which was to be brought up to the full strength of 286,000 men authorized by the National Defense Act. This was to be boosted by the National Guard, raised to its maximum authorized strength of about 450,000 men, and by the National Army created in two 500,000-man sections whenever the

president decided. In fact, these three parts of the army never really existed, especially in the A.E.F. Recruits and conscripts were generally absorbed without discrimination into those units that needed men, and this fact was recognized in the middle of 1918 by the War Department, which ordered that all land forces would be part of the U.S. Army. It was only in the organization of the army that the original segments were still apparent, for numbers up to 25 were originally reserved for regular army divisions, those between 26 and 75 for National Guard divisions, and those from 76 upward for National Army divisions.

Pershing's need for 1,000,000 men in France as an initial step was based on the concept of an independent American fighting force of 20 divisions and their supporting units. Working from Pershing's baseline figures, the War Department evolved a scheme to send to France by the end of 1918 a force of 30 first-line divisions, which with their supporting units would total 1,372,000 men.

Then came the major disasters of 1917, and Pershing revised his figures upward. In June 1917, the A.E.F. commander reported that he needed 3,000,000 men in 66 divisions by May 1919. Further recommendations, following in short order, were for 80 divisions by April 1919 and 100 divisions by July 1919.

The War Department felt that 100 divisions would probably be beyond American capabilities and possibly too much for Pershing's needs. But after conducting its own study, the War Department finalized a need for 98 divisions, of which 80 should be in France by the summer of 1919. As a first step toward this larger army, the original aim of 30 divisions in France by the end of 1918 was increased to 52 divisions by the same time.

Powerful American Formation

It is worth noting that the number of divisions is perhaps a misleading way of judging the size of the projected American army, for at a strength of nearly 28,000 men, American divisions had almost

Training in the United States itself was not without its upsets and accidents. This observation balloon crashed in flames at Fort Sill, Oklahoma.

National Guard
For further references see pages
14, 15, 24, 128, 130

the number of men in Allied and German divisions. The size of the American division resulted from one of Pershing's first recommendations from France, where he saw the need for a basic formation possessing both great striking power and great staying power. Working from Pershing's recommendations, the War Department evolved a structure that gave the division about the same strength as a corps in the Civil War.

The American division included two brigades, each made up of two infantry regiments and one machine gun battalion, one divisional machine gun battalion, one field artillery brigade made up of one heavy and two light regiments, one combat engineer regiment, and support elements such as signal and medical units.

The army's peak strength in World War I was just over 3,685,000 men formed into 62 divisions, of which 43 were despatched overseas. In short, at the time of the war's end in November 1918, the army was close to its schedule for 52 divisions in France by the end of 1918.

Planning and Administration: The Essential Tools

These expansion plans were very ambitious. They depended for their eventual success on planning and administration of a very high quality in the provision of accommodation, uniforms, weapons, equipment, and supplies. In the early part of the program, new regiments and other units of the regular army were created almost immediately, using existing accommodation, while new National Guard regiments were created in two segments and housed in huge tent camps, mainly in the warm southern states. The first draft registrations were completed in June 1917, but it was September of the same year before the first men were called; the interval was used for a crash building program for the camps for the National

Above: Two U.S. Marine Corps sergeants display the finer details of combat training.

Left: Men of the U.S. Marine Corps practice with a Lewis gun. The government bought only 2,500 of these light machine guns in 0·3-inch caliber for operational use. They were allocated to the Marine Corps and the Navy.

The drafting of workers into the armed forces brought many women into parts of industry that had previously been male preserves. Typical of this important economic and social movement is this woman welder in a U.S. arsenal.

Army. This was a major success for the Quartermaster Corps' Cantonment Division, which worked with the civilian Committee on Emergency Construction.

The production of weapons, munitions, and other supplies was an even greater problem, for in addition to the army's requirements, there were orders from the navy and existing contracts from the European Allies to be met. As the men who framed the National Defense Act had envisaged, this demanded full economic mobilization. The National Defense Act had provided a Council of National Defense, which formed the basis of central planning and control. As one of its first moves, this council created the Munitions Standards Board, an industry body to set standards for munitions manufacture. It grew steadily to become the War Industries Board, which coordinated all purchasing by army and navy agencies, established production priorities, created new plants and converted existing facilities to priority tasks, and coordinated the efforts of various civilian war agencies.

The movement of so many troops and so much equipment inside the United States, and then to their embarkation ports, was a complex and demanding task for the nation's railroads. The government therefore set up the Railway War Board, which became the Railroad Administration under eventual government control. Shipping also remained a problem, despite the creation of the Shipping Board in 1916. In an effort to conserve shipping for military purposes, the government cut imports, established a mass construction program for standardized cargo vessels, and seized interned German ships. Even so, British ships had to handle much of the American traffic across the Atlantic.

The demands on American industry were so great and so immediate that they would in themselves have posed great problems. Added to these difficulties were the time needed for contracts to be let and for plants to be retooled. This meant a considerable delay before American weapons could reach American troops, although in the short term, it was acceptable for the new units to train with obsolete weapons or even wooden dummies. For the growing number of field formations, however, there was no alternative to the use of existing weapons that could be supplied by the European Allies, most notably France and the United Kingdom.

Weapon Shortages

Rifles were the only weapons that were not a problem, for production of the Springfield Model 1903 was increased rapidly by army arsenals, and plants that were making the British Lee-Enfield were able to modify this excellent rifle to take American ammunition. Initially, all of the A.E.F.'s automatic rifles and machine guns were supplied by the Allies, but from mid-1918, the superb Browning automatic rifle and machine gun began to pour from American production lines in large quantities. The problem of artillery was more difficult; of the 2,250 pieces of artillery used by the A.E.F., only 100 were of American manufacture. The same was true of tanks and aircraft, and while the U.S. Tank Corps used mainly French

The Mitrailleuse Saint Etienne Modele 1907 was not a particularly effective weapon and was notoriously unreliable. It had been developed from the Puteaux Modele 1905, which itself had been an attempt to create in a state arsenal an improved version of the commercial Hotchkiss medium machine gun. Fed by 24–or 30-round metal clips and weighing 56·75 pounds, the air-cooled Mle 1907 fired its 8-mm bullets with a muzzle velocity of 2,300 feet per second at a cyclic rate of between 400 and 600 rounds per minute. Limited numbers of this weapon were used by American battalions attached to French divisions.

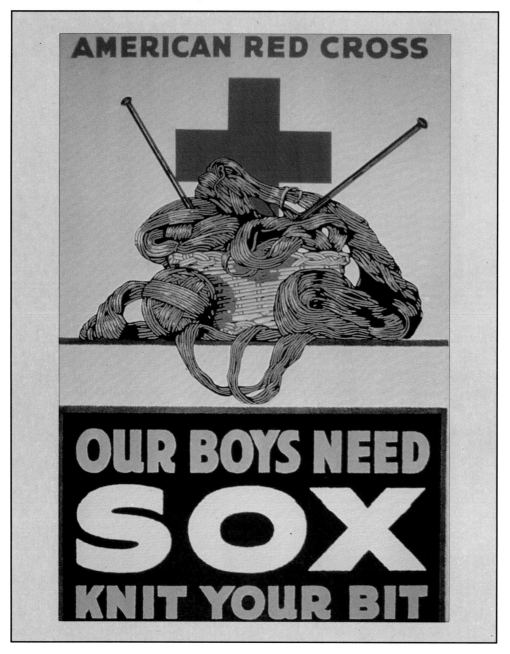

AMERICAN RED CROSS

OUR BOYS NEED SOX KNIT YOUR BIT

An American Red Cross poster of World War I.

tanks, the Air Section used a miscellany of British, French, and Italian aircraft.

Matters were easier with the soldiers' personal kit and food. The army liaised closely with the War Food Administration to make sure that there were none of the shortages and contract abuses that had marked earlier American wars, and the draft was kept down to the rate at which inductees could be provided with uniforms and other items of personal kit. There were occasional difficulties, but they resulted not from industry failures,

but from the clumsy contracting system of the Quartermaster Corps, which soon revised its way of doing things.

Another difficult requirement was finding enough officers. In April 1917, the army had an immediate need for 200,000 officers, but had only 9,000. The General Staff at first thought that the best solution was to spread these commissioned and non commissioned officers through the enlarging army as cadres, but soon saw that the regulars would be lost in the vast growth and have no real effect. In earlier

A war loan poster of World War I. The first Liberty Loan bonds were issued on May 2, 1917, and this initial issue was followed by three more drives (in October 1917, April 1918, and October 1918) and a Victory Loan drive of 1919. Bonds were sold in denominations between $50 and $100,000, and the five drives raised a total of $21 billion.

American wars, most notably the Civil War, officers had been appointed directly from civilian life, but this practice was not followed in World War I except in the case of doctors and technical specialists.

An Effective Officer Training Program

The first expansion of the officer corps was provided by 16 Officers' Training Camps, where civilians and reservists were evaluated, the unsuitable weeded out, and those with potential trained. In the longer terms, suitable enlisted men in the regular army were commissioned, and others emerged from the Reserve Officers' Training Corps, and a Student Army Training Corps at colleges and universities. However, the largest number of officers was produced by Officers' Training Camps in divisional cantonments, and later from eight Officers' Training Schools. Candidates were admitted to these OTSs only after careful screening,

Marine, U.S. Marine Corps, Western Front, France, 1918

By the beginning of World War I, the U.S. Marine Corps had already developed a reputation as an elite military organization. The corps specialized in overseas operations and was particularly proud of its allegiance to the navy rather than to the army. So it was natural that the corps should provide an early contingent for the American Expeditionary Force. The 2nd Division included the 4th (Marine) Brigade, which included the 5th and 6th Marine Regiments supported by the 6th Marine Machine Gun Battalion. Uniforms and equipment were similar to those of the army, but had important differences of detail. These differences became reduced as marines in France were resupplied from army stocks. Among this marine's equipment are the M1903/05 Springfield rifle of 0·30-06-inch caliber with a no-buckle webbing sling, a cartridge belt based on the U.S. Army's M1910 item with ten pouches each holding two five-round clips, a light cotton bandolier with five pouches each holding two five-round clips, an M1917 helmet of manganese steel with an oilcloth interior lining and brown leather chinstrap, M1917 ankle boots, and puttees of olive drab cloth. Other items would have been a "Liberty light" flashlight, an M1910 first aid pouch, an M1910 canteen and carrier, an M1917 trench knife with a wooden handle, knuckleduster guard and triangular-section blade, an M1905 bayonet in an M1910 fabric and leather scabbard, and an M1917 gas mask copied from the British "small box respirator."

and underwent a period of three months' intensive training before the successful 60 percent were commissioned into the National Army.

The enlisted soldiers also received intensive training in the United States before they were sent overseas. There was considerable argument about the length of this training period, but the War Department finally set it at four months. This length of time proved wholly inadequate, because newly trained soldiers arrived in similarly inexperienced formations, and Pershing established a program of severe divisional training for each formation as it arrived in France. This program, undertaken with the assistance of teams of combat-experienced British and French troops, was long enough to cause criticism, not only from Allied officers who wanted to see the American divisions in the line, but also from some impatient American officers.

World War I was a vast conflict requiring technical and logistical solutions previously not even imagined. So it was inevitable that the American effort to build up its organization should be found wanting in some areas, and that historic institutions should have to be modified. Two places in which World War I had such an effect were the authority of the chief of staff and the organization of the General Staff.

March: An Excellent Chief of Staff

For reasons of national and army politics, the office of chief of staff had not had a notably strong holder up to this time. This situation changed in March 1918, when, at the instigation of Secretary of War Newton D. Baker, the War Department appointed Major General Peyton C. March to the position. Recalled from France, where he had been Pershing's chief of artillery, March was promoted to full general and agreed with Baker that a thorough overhaul of the General Staff was needed to remove a number of problems that had been discovered in the quartermaster, supply, and transportation departments.

The tool March needed for this task was the Overman Act of May 1918, which

gave the president wide-ranging authority to reorganize executive agencies during the emergency situation presented by the war. March was therefore given permission to establish the chief of staff's supremacy over the various bureau heads. March declared that the bureau heads were from that time subordinate to the chief of staff, and that they were to report to the secretary of war only through the chief of staff.

This was only a first step in March's complete restructuring of the General Staff, in which four main divisions were created as the War Plans; Military Intelligence; Operations; and Purchase, Storage, and Traffic Divisions. The War Plans and Operations divisions shared the functions previously undertaken by the War College, and in the Purchase, Storage, and Transport Division, the army finally achieved control over its own logistics. Evidence of the General Staff's new importance is provided by the growth of its strength to slightly more than 1,000 men.

Newton D. Baker held the all-important post of Secretary of War during World War I.

John Pershing
For further references
see pages
21, 22, 24, 25, 26, *34*,
35, 39, 40, 41, 52, 54,
59, 60, *61*, 63, 64, 65,
67, 77, 79, 82, 87, 88,
92, 93, 95, 99, 101, 106,
107, 110, 111, 113, *130*

Recalled from France, where he had served as Pershing's chief of artillery in the rank of major general, Peyton C. March became the U.S. Army Chief of Staff and, with the rank of general, a major element in the creation of the modern U.S. Army.

The only hindrance to the overall supremacy of the chief of staff was Pershing, who as field commander in France had been promoted to full general before March had. Pershing steadily refused March's efforts to assert his authority in France. The secretary of war frequently found himself forced to act as arbiter between the two generals, and he usually sided with Pershing, who continued to run the A.E.F. almost as a separate empire. It was only after the end of World War I, when Pershing returned to the United States and succeeded March as chief of staff, that the dilemma was removed.

Cooperation with the Allies

When Pershing left the United States for France, his orders included the instruction "to cooperate with the forces of the other countries...but in so doing the underlying idea must be kept in view that the forces of the United States are a separate and distinct component of the combined forces, the identity of which must be preserved." Pershing agreed fully with this instruction, which brought the American commander into considerable political conflict with his Allied counterparts at a time when they had exhausted virtually all their manpower reserves.

The Allied commanders were not confident of the ability of the inexperienced Americans to undertake independent or even coordinated operations. Instead, they thought that the best way to employ the A.E.F. was as a pool of fresh formations to reinforce existing Allied corps and armies. The Allied argument was that they possessed experienced staffs and commanders, as well as the necessary artillery, aviation, and tank support elements, but lacked manpower. The Americans, the Allies pointed out, were in exactly the opposite position, and

General Tasker Howard Bliss had been U.S. Army Chief of Staff for a short period, but now played an important part as the American representative to the Allies' Supreme War Council.

it therefore made sense to combine Allied expertise and heavy weapons with American manpower to recreate effective combat formations.

Pershing steadily refused to entertain the notion, and when the Allied leaders, David Lloyd George of the United Kingdom and Georges Clemenceau of France, went over his head to Washington, Baker and Wilson supported Pershing without hesitation. Another avenue of approach to the Americans was provided by General Tasker H. Bliss, previously chief of staff and currently the American representative on the Supreme War Council. Bliss was more conciliatory than Pershing and the American government, but still refused to consider the subordination of American forces to foreign command.

Early in 1918, the British offered to provide the transport for 150 American battalions of infantry so that they might be used to strengthen British divisions that had been reduced in strength from 12 to nine battalions. The British offer suggested that the American units would be returned to American command in four or five months. Pershing again refused, but seeing that transport difficulties were slowing the growth of the A.E.F., he suggested that the British transport capability be used for the movement of whole American divisions. The British realized that this meant the movement of only three divisions with 36 infantry battalions, and therefore refused. However, it was later decided that the British would move six divisions without heavy equipment on the condition that the divisions were then assembled, outfitted, and trained in the British zone. This program eventually saw the delivery of 10 American divisions.

The Americans Assemble

Pershing chose to assemble the A.E.F. in the Lorraine region southeast of Paris and east of Verdun, and he established his headquarters at Chaumont, near the source of the Marne River, in a region well away from the areas where the British and French operated in their heaviest concentrations. The British were concerned with Belgium and northern France, and the French with the eastern arc around

A lighthearted moment before departure for France as U.S. Marines dance with visitors to their battleship in 1918.

Paris, effectively tying up the strategic opportunities and communications of these areas. Farther south, Pershing concluded, there were still areas of strategic opportunity, including German coal and iron mining regions, and some of Germany's most important lateral railroads. In addition, his lines of communications could make use of the railroads of southern and southwestern France, which were not already highly committed to the efforts of the Allies and therefore available to connect the Americans with ports such as Bordeaux and Marseilles.

At the beginning of 1918, two more American divisions were scheduled for early arrival in France. However, the Allies felt that the pace of the American build up in overall strength and operational capability was slow. Drained by the disastrous campaigns of 1917, the armies of France and the United Kingdom were now faced with a period of defensive operations until sizable American forces were ready for action. This defensive posture was made all the more necessary by the loss of Russia after the Soviet revolution of November 1917. In December 1917, the new government signed the armistice of Brest Litovsk, which erased Russia from the Allied ranks and freed substantial German forces for redeployment elsewhere, most notably on the Western Front. However, the Brest Litovsk armi-

Left: One of the major ports of arrival for American troops in France was the Breton city of Brest. When deep-water berths were not available, the American troops were carried ashore in lighters such as this.

Below: World War I was the first war in which the United States was involved to be covered in detail by movie as well as still cameras. This is an official U.S. Marine Corps crew filming the loading of a ship bound for France.

Above: Many U.S. troops staged through the United Kingdom on their way to France. This column of American soldiers is marching south over Westminster Bridge in London, with the Houses of Parliament in the background, during 1918.

Right: U.S. soldiers disembark in Brest, northwestern France, on July 22, 1918

stice did not end hostilities between Russia and Germany. Fighting resumed in February 1918, and continued operations kept 80 German divisions on the Eastern Front.

Germany's Bold Plan

Germany's military leaders, General Erich Ludendorff and his notional superior, Field Marshal Paul von Hindenburg, were fully aware that the Western Front was the decisive theater, and that Germany's sole hope of winning the war now depended on the destruction of the British and French armies before the full weight of American aid was available later in 1918. The troops already on the Western Front were bolstered by divisions from the Eastern Front and even some recalled from Italy to a strength of some 3,500,000 men in 192 divisions. Ludendorff planned to attack the British on the Somme River sector with 62 divisions early in spring, with the intention of pushing back their right wing and forcing them to pull back toward the English Channel. With the Allies divided, the Germans would next strike at the French on the Aisne River sector.

The German drives to the west began on March 21, 1918, with an attack on two British armies by three German armies. At first, the Germans made sweeping gains, especially against the British 5th Army, which had only recently taken over this southernmost British sector from the French. However, the British 3rd Army on its left flank fared better, and by the end of the month the Germans were running out of strength and impetus. The British were furious at the lack of French support, and rightly claimed that Marshal Henri Petain was more concerned with protecting Paris than maintaining the Allied front line. Field Marshal Sir Douglas Haig, commanding the British Expeditionary Force, urged General Sir Henry Wilson, the British chief of staff, to recommend the appointment of ''Foch or some other French general who will fight'' as Allied supreme commander. On March 26, General (soon Marshal) Ferdinand Foch was appointed Allied coordinator for the Western Front by an emergency

meeting of the Supreme War Council, and on April 3 he became Allied supreme commander in France. This was a singularly important development for the Allies. The supreme commander's position was not as potent as it could have been, however, as Foch was limited to ''strategic direction,'' while national commanders retained ''tactical control.''

Pershing agreed in principle with this move, and had already responded to the Allied crisis with the offer of eight American divisions on March 27.

The Action at Seicheprey

During this period, American troops became involved in their first major action, which occurred on April 20 in an otherwise quiet sector of the front in Lorraine, close to the town of St. Mihiel. Here, the 26th Division came under a short but severe artillery bombardment, followed by a German regimental-size infantry attack intended to take the village of Seicheprey. The Germans boxed in the American defenders with artillery barrages and took the village during the morning. During

Field Marshal Paul von Hindenburg (left) and General Erich Ludendorff were the team that led the German military machine through most of World War I's later stages.

Paul von Hindenburg
For further references see pages 96, 102, 103, 116

Erich Ludendorff
For further references see pages 40, 41, 51, 52, 56, 57, 59, 72, 76, 81, 96, 97, 101, 102, 103, 113, 114, 116

An American observation balloon at Camp de Souge near Bordeaux in 1918, with the winch vehicle on the left, and the observer's basket in the center surrounded by ground handlers. These hydrogen-filled, and therefore highly flammable, balloons were vital to front-line operations. They provided a stable platform from which the observer could see the enemy's trenches and all movement in and around them, and also watch where his own artillery's fire fell. The basket contained the airborne part of a telephone system used by the observer to relay corrections to the battery for which he was spotting. Because of their tactical importance, balloons were very well protected by ground-based light antiaircraft guns and machine guns, and they could be hauled down quickly. On each side, however, there were pilots who specialized in the hazardous task of ''balloon busting,'' and observers had to be prepared to parachute out of blazing balloons.

the afternoon, however, the Americans counterattacked and retook Seicheprey. Throughout the rest of the day, the Germans held a nearby wood, but the American infantrymen, scattered and cut off by the day's fighting, regrouped in the night and drove the Germans out of the wood on the following day. The German casualties included 160 dead, while the Americans suffered 634 casualties, not counting 136 men captured.

During the crisis of these weeks, Pershing was faced with renewed Allied pressure for the use of his divisions to reinforce the exhausted Allied armies. Pershing's offer of eight divisions for the duration of the crisis had been followed by a flurry of high-level communications, but in the end the American commander's position was maintained by the government, and Allied commanders decided that the best thing was to create the required American army as rapidly as possible.

Ludendorff's first offensive failed in its task of pushing the British back toward the English Channel, even with the aid of a secondary offensive launched on April 9 in the Lys River sector. The German commander pushed ahead with his strategic plan, however. He felt that this was the only option open to the Germans, but

realized that it was essential to split the British and French before either of them could be defeated. Thus the second great offensive, by two German armies against a single French army from May 27 on the Aisne River sector, was a diversion designed to draw Allied reserves into this sector before the Germans attacked the British once more.

The German offensive succeeded beyond Ludendorff's expectations, and moved so menacingly toward Paris that Pershing offered Foch the use of five American divisions on the Marne River sector. Foch accepted the offer eagerly, and by May 31, the advance elements of Major General Omar Bundy's 2nd Division and Major General J.T. Dickman's 3rd Division were moving up to bolster General Denis Duchene's French 6th Army.

The Battle of Cantigny

Meanwhile, American troops had under-taken their first offensive operation of the war on May 28, the capture of Cantigny by Major General Robert Lee Bullard's 1st Division. Planned as the start of a French offensive against the Amiens salient, it was also the Americans' first operation in divisional strength. It took place some 50 miles to the northwest, in the sector held by General Eugene Debeny's French 1st Army.

Lying on high ground, Cantigny was a well-fortified village used as an observation point by the seasoned troops of General Oscar von Hutier's German 18th Army. Supported by American and French artillery, as well as by French tanks, the division committed one regiment to the initial attack on May 28. Maneuvering with speed and skill, the regiment took the village early in the morning, and then held on with grim skill and determination as the Germans threw on counterattack after counterattack right into the next day. American losses in this local, but morale-boosting, action were 1,607 men, including 199 killed.

Red Cross volunteers hand out cigarettes and chocolate to American soldiers on their way to the front near Montmirail on May 31, 1918.

Ferdinand Foch
For further references see pages 39, 51, 52, 56, 59, 60, 61, 63, 65, 67, 76, 79, 80, 82, 113

Right: The success of the U.S. Marine Corps in the Battle of Belleau Wood was greeted with great acclaim in the United States. Here, two admiring children wear the cap and badge of the corps.

Below: An American trench and command post at Cantigny, where the U.S. Army launched its first offensive action of World War I.

The victory was not exploited as had been planned. The French called off their intended offensive because of the deteriorating position along the Aisne River sector. Even so, the Battle of Cantigny was an American success that pointed the way to greater things in the near future.

The Battle of Chateau-Thierry

Much can be said of the Battle of Chateau-Thierry. The 2nd and 3rd Divisions began to arrive at Meaux on the Aisne River behind the French front on the night of May 30/31, and the leading elements of these two American formations were immediately thrown into the effort against the tip of the German offensive. By May 31, a machine gun battalion of the 3rd Division had been moved up by truck to reinforce the French at Chateau-Thierry, where the Germans were close to securing a bridgehead over the Marne. The American machine gunners proved decisive in holding the bridges across the river and repulsing the German effort. The rest of the division

American troops on board the *Cuba* after disembarking from the *Mauritania* in Brest harbor. American soldiers continued to flood across the North Atlantic right up to the end of the war, reinforcing the already large American forces in France in case the war lasted into 1919, as most senior commanders expected.

Right: American soldiers man a Hotchkiss 8-mm medium machine gun in the antiaircraft role during the Battle of Chateau-Thierry. This French weapon was heavy and cumbersome, but these factors were not important in the AA role, where the weapon's reliability combined with it's accuracy, rate of fire, and range to produce a moderately effective gun.

Below: Men of the 11th Infantry Regiment, 28th Division, rest near Chateau-Thierry on July 21, 1918.

Left: The town of Chateau-Thierry came in for very rough handling as the French and Americans checked the German advance on the Marne River during June 1918.

Below: French school children watch an ammunition train moving up to the front through the village of Soulosse on April 10, 1918.

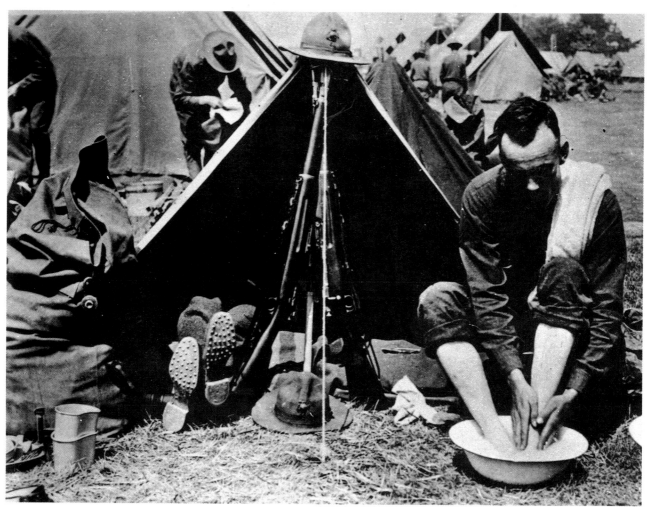

Conditions of warfare in France during World War I made great demands on the soldiers' feet, and at the same time made it difficult to look after them and avoid conditions such as trench foot. One of the signs of a good officer was that he inspected the feet of his men and made sure they washed and dried their feet properly on a regular basis. This is a marine in a camp behind the front.

soon arrived. Joining forces with the rallying French infantry, the 3rd Division helped drive the Germans back across the river at Jaulgonne, slightly to the east of Chateau-Thierry.

On May 29, the 2nd Division's two infantry brigades (one army and one marine) moved into the line to the left of the 3rd Division, replacing the French XXI Corps between Vaux and Belleau. Here they checked the German advance from Chateau-Thierry toward Paris via Vaux in two days of hard fighting.

The Battle of Belleau Wood

The first sustained attack by American forces in World War I, generally known as the Battle of Belleau Wood, took place in the closing stages of the Germans' Aisne River offensive. Belleau, a village just north of Chateau-Thierry, lay at the

tip of the salient driven toward Paris by the German 7th Army. Captured by the Germans on June 3, it marked the center of the sector held by the defending Allied force, the French 6th Army, supported by the American 2nd and 3rd Divisions.

The Allied command felt that the momentum of the German offensive was slackening noticeably and would be halted by a determined counterattack on the French 6th Army's sector. The 2nd Division was therefore committed to an attack to take the large village of Bouresches and the Bois de Belleau (Belleau Wood), which lay between Bouresches and the village of Belleau about one mile to the northwest.

The detailed planning for the attack was carried out at the headquarters of the 2nd Division, located in La Voie du Chatel, about a mile behind the front that had stabilized between June 1 and 5. The Battle of Belleau Wood began on June 6,

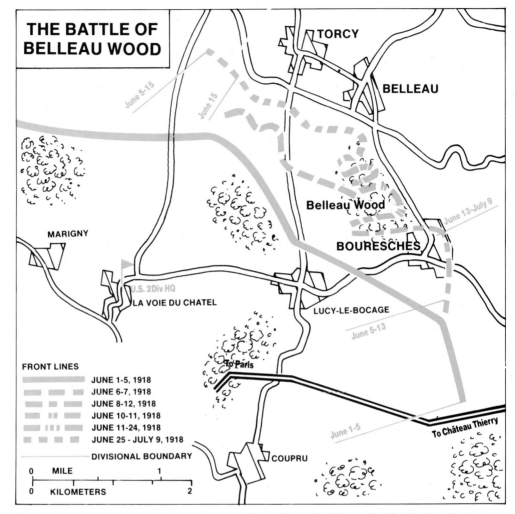

Belleau Wood
For further references see pages
42, 46, *48, 49, 50,* 51, *52, 58*

THE BATTLE OF BELLEAU WOOD

TORCY

BELLEAU

June 5-15

June 15

Belleau Wood

June 13-July 9

BOURESCHES

MARIGNY

U.S. 2Div HQ

LA VOIE DU CHATEL

LUCY-LE-BOCAGE

June 5-13

To Paris

FRONT LINES

	JUNE 1-5, 1918
	JUNE 6-7, 1918
	JUNE 8-12, 1918
	JUNE 10-11, 1918
	JUNE 11-24, 1918
	JUNE 25 - JULY 9, 1918

DIVISIONAL BOUNDARY

To Château Thierry

June 1-5

COUPRU

0 MILE 1

0 KILOMETERS 2

ARRAS

Somme

AMIENS

MONTDIDIER

ST QUENTIN

BELGIUM

Sambre

Oise

Front line, June 5, 1918

SOISSONS

Marne

Belleau Wood

MEZIERES

SEDAN

CHANTEAU THIERRY

ÉPERNAY

Aisne

Meuse

Seine

CHALONS

F R A N C E

VERDUN

ST. MIHIEL

0 MILES 50

0 KILOMETERS 80

THE BATTLE OF BELLEAU WOOD

when the 5th and 6th Marine Regiments advanced against the German forces in Bouresches and the wood. In three days of bitter fighting, the marines managed to push their positions forward about 400 yards on the left, toward the village of Belleau, and about 800 yards on the right, into the edge of the wood on the western outskirts of Bouresches.

Late on June 8, this initial effort was halted as the marines pulled back to regroup. The 2nd Division now decided to switch the main effort to the right, and between June 9 and 12, the Americans took most of Bouresches. On June 10 and 11, other American regiments managed to drive into the southeastern part of Belleau Wood, almost as far as the road connecting Bouresches with Belleau, but could not link up with the forces in Bouresches. From June 11, the 2nd Division was reinforced by elements of the 3rd Division, which allowed the

Cheerful marines rest on their way forward to Belleau Wood.

Marines in the very difficult fighting terrain of Belleau Wood.

Marines capture a German machine-gun nest in the Belleau Wood fighting.

Close-quarter action as the marines take the fight to the Germans in Belleau Wood.

Marines with a German trench mortar captured at Belleau Wood.

The villages around Belleau Wood suffered severe damage during the concentrated fighting for the area.

Americans to seize another enclave in Belleau Wood, just northwest of the original enclave, between June 11 and 24. Toward the end of this time, the German defense began to fail. By June 25, the Americans had linked up the three enclaves in Bouresches and Belleau Wood and extended their left wing northwest, past the southern side of Belleau toward the village of Torcy.

In the fighting, the Germans lost 9,500 men killed and wounded, as well as another 1,600 taken prisoner. By the standards of the time, the Battle of Belleau Wood was a small-scale affair, but it had provided the American forces with an excellent and successful chance to test their capabilities. At the same time, it had shown the Allies that the Americans could fight and win, and had also given the Germans unpalatable food for thought about the consequences when large numbers of American divisions started to fight on the Western Front.

The Germans in a Poor Overall Position

The Germans now held three salients into the Allied line. It was not a situation with which Ludendorff was happy, even though the two most southerly ones did threaten Franco-British cohesion and point the way to Paris. At the same time, they had exhausted most of Ludendorff's offensive strength and left the German forces with a longer front line to be defended. Yet the first three German offensives had considerably unsettled the French, and Clemenceau needed all his formidable ferocity to quell the defeatists in the French government. Foch and Petain thought that the British should shift major forces south from Flanders and Artois to help protect the French capital. Such a move was vetoed by Haig, one of the few senior Allied commanders who had realized that the German Aisne

Sir Douglas Haig
For further references see pages
39, 52, 59, 65, 67

The art of camouflage became very important in World War I. These are American ambulance trucks near Neuville.

A French 37-mm trench howitzer of the HQ Company, 6th Marine Regiment, in action against German positions in the Battle of Belleau Wood.

River operation was a diversion intended do just what Foch and Petain were now suggesting. Foch finally agreed with the logic of Haig's position, and decided that the British should remain where they were.

However, the Allied position northeast of Paris did have to be strengthened. The Americans would clearly have to enter the fight much sooner than Pershing had planned.

On the other side of the front line, Ludendorff had been planning his next move. The German commander decided that a fourth offensive had to be mounted as quickly as possible on the sides of the Allied salient that had been created between the positions created by the German first and third offensives. Running across the upper reaches of the Oise River between Soissons and Montdidier, this Allied position threatened Germany's only line of railroad communication into the Aisne/Marne River salient created by the

third offensive. Ludendorff's plan was therefore based on a pair of offensives: the German 18th Army was to attack southwest from the Somme River salient, while the German 7th Army was to move west from the Aisne River salient. Ludendorff expected that the two armies would meet in the region of Compiegne on the Oise River, thereby eliminating the Allied salient between the two German salients. With their forces on the line from Montdidier to Chateau-Thierry via Compiegne, the Germans would have secure communications into the sector and would again be threatening Paris.

This, Ludendorff hoped, would persuade the Allies to reinforce the defenses of Paris by moving troops from other parts of the Western Front while the Germans were moving divisions away from this sector to the Flanders front, which the German commander believed to be the decisive sector.

The German preparations were pushed

through with great speed. In fact, the planning was so open that many Allied commanders feared that they were a feint to distract attention from secret preparations that might be taking place in Flanders, well to the north. By this time, however, German soldiers, deserting from the army at an increasing rate, were able to confirm that the preparations were for a real, not a dummy, offensive. These deserters also provided information about attack points, dates, and times.

Allied Plans Postponed

Since May 20, Foch had been planning a series of strategic counteroffensives by the Allied armies, but they were suspended in the light of German intentions. The French organized their defense in depth; just before the time set for the Germans' preparatory bombardment on June 8, they laid down their own heavy artillery bombardment. The German offensive was somewhat blunted,

An American sailor befriends a French refugee orphan in 1918.

but nevertheless broke through the first French defenses. However, it then began to stumble as it met sustained resistance. The Germans continued to advance until June 11, but on June 12, they were halted by the French, who had significant American assistance. A lull settled along the Western Front at the end of June after this German fourth offensive had been checked. During this period, the French 10th Army launched a small but successful offensive against the western side of the Germans' Aisne River salient to the west of Soissons. This drive helped to keep Foch's offensive plans alive at a time when the Germans had the strategic initiative. It also laid the groundwork for the first major Allied counteroffensive, which was launched in mid-July – after a delay occasioned by the German fifth offensive.

During the lull, Pershing was able to announce, on July 4, that there were now 1,000,000 Americans in France, the personnel of 19 divisions. These forces included nine divisions that had gained some combat experience, mainly in secondary theaters; two that were completing their training; and eight that had recently arrived and were in the earlier stages of their training. American troops were now arriving at the rate of 250,000 a month. Shortly before this time, Pershing had followed Allied practice and created the first American corps headquarters. Major General Hunter Liggett's I Corps assumed responsibility for the sector around Chateau-Thierry; Major General George W. Read's II Corps had the 27th and 30th Divisions under command and fought the rest of the war with the British Expeditionary Force; and Major General

Private Harry Shelby is decorated by King George V for his gallantry in the advance at Hamel on July 4, 1918. Standing behind the table is General John Pershing.

Robert L. Bullard
For further references
see pages
41, 111, 113

Robert L. Bullard's III Corps had not yet taken control of a sector of the front line.

Ludendorff was still convinced during this period that the major German effort had to be made against the British in Flanders, but he decided that a last diversionary effort had to be made first farther south. The sector he chose was centered on Reims. This Champagne/Marne River offensive, the fifth great German offensive of 1918, was scheduled for mid-July. The plan was for the German 7th Army to advance up the Marne through Epernay to Chalons, where it would link up with the German 3rd Army attacking south. A successful offensive would pinch out the heavily fortified Reims area and, Ludendorff hoped, draw Allied divisions from the north.

American Support for the French

The Allied command was warned by German preparations and its own aerial reconnaissance, and the details were again confirmed by German deserters.

The start of the German offensive, on July 15, was again spoiled by a French artillery bombardment, and the Germans made only slight gains in two areas before the offensive was checked on July 17. The major gains were made by the German 7th Army against the French 9th and 5th Armies on the Marne River sector, where the French were ably reinforced by the 3rd, 26th "Yankee," 28th, and 42nd "Rainbow" Divisions. Again, the 3rd Division particularly distinguished itself east of Chateau-Thierry. Its 38th Infantry Regiment fought a determined defensive battle on three fronts and completely blunted the German drive in its area.

Even as the last German offensive unfolded its weary course, Foch was finalizing the details of the Allied strategic counteroffensives and assembling the necessary divisions in the appropriate sectors. The first element of these drives was designed to capitalize on the French 10th Army's fairly small-scale operation of June. It envisaged an attack all around the Marne River salient, though the main emphasis was placed on the 10th Army,

Another French warplane used by the United States in France was the Breguet Bre.14 two-seater, which was delivered in two forms, as a bomber and as a reconnaissance aircraft. Here, the rear seat is occupied by a Signal Corps officer with a movie camera.

on the salient's western side, to cut the road between Soissons and Chateau-Thierry, the main supply route for the German forces in the Marne River salient. If this western effort was successful, the plan was to develop it immediately into a general offensive to reduce the complete salient.

The salient was held by the 9th and 7th Armies of the German Army Group "Kronprinz Wilhelm." The attacking forces included the 10th and 6th Armies of the French Army Group "Fayolle" in the west, and the 9th and 5th Armies of the French Army Group "Maistre" in the east. American divisions were allocated major parts in the operation, although only under French command. In the west, the 1st and 2nd Divisions, plus part of the 4th Division, were allocated to the 10th Army. Moving counterclockwise around the salient, the French 6th Army could draw on the support of another part of the 4th Division as well

as the 26th Division, and the French 9th Army included the 3rd Division. There were no American divisions in the 5th Army, but as the offensive continued, other American divisions became involved and were employed under American corps control. In the 6th Army's sector, for example, the 4th and 42nd Divisions were used under the command of I Corps. In the 9th Army's sector, the 28th and 32nd Divisions were employed under III Corps.

The Aisne-Marne Offensive

The offensive known as the Aisne-Marne offensive began on July 18. Ludendorff was away in Flanders planning the proposed offensive by the German Army Group "Rupprecht," and as an eloquent testimony of the Allied success in the first two days of the offensive, Ludendorff cancelled the Flanders operation on July 20. The fighting itself was fairly routine.

Mail from home played a particularly important part in keeping up the morale of fighting men in France. This is a mail delivery at a U.S. Marine Corps unit in the front line.

On the first day, the Allies made significant gains. On the second, German resistance stiffened, although on that day, the German 7th Army abandoned its bridgehead across the Marne. From July 21, the German command realized that a continued attempt to hold the salient would be a complete waste of manpower and materiel, and therefore ordered a steady withdrawal to the line of the Aisne and Vesle Rivers. This retreat was carried out with great skill under cover of artillery and machine-gun rearguards, and the German air arm slowed down the Allied advance with ground-attack missions.

By August 6, the salient had disappeared after an Allied advance of about 20 miles. Paris was no longer under German threat, the important railroad line between Chalons and Paris had been reopened, and the French and Americans now occupied a line that was 28 miles shorter than that of July 18. Just as important, the offensive had shown that despite losses of more than 50,000 men, the soldiers of four countries (France, the United States, the United Kingdom, and

Italy) could fight an effective cooperative battle under unified command. As a result, Allied morale was boosted considerably.

On the other side of the wire, the offensive had cost the Germans large numbers of casualties, as well as 30,000 men taken prisoner. More than 600 guns, 200 trench mortars, and 3,000 machine guns had been lost by the Germans. In addition to these heavy physical losses, the disaster of the Marne River salient was a terrible blow to German morale.

The part played by the American divisions was significant, but was so complicated in its territorial extent that the accompanying map on page 59 describes their efforts considerably more accurately than words. Yet it is illuminating to look at the two American divisions that formed part of the Allied spearhead, the French 10th Army. The 1st Division remained in the line up to July 28 and advanced on a line very slightly south of east, to a point just north of Buzancy. The division encountered seven German divisions, and while suffering the loss of 7,000 men

The American advances in the Aisne-Marne offensive.

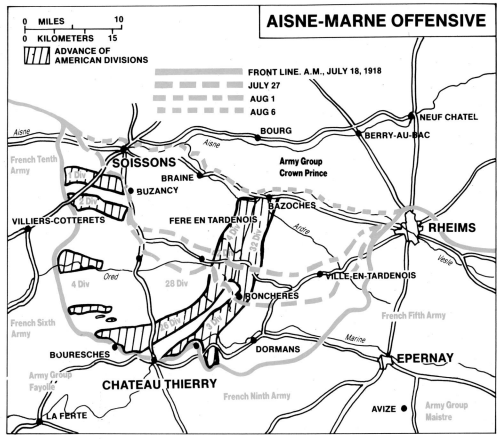

(1,000 killed and 6,000 wounded), it took 3,800 prisoners and captured 70 guns. The 2nd Division remained in the line until July 20. It advanced on a line parallel to, but slightly south of, the 1st Division's line. The division reached Tigny and, in spite of suffering a total of 5,000 casualties, captured 3,000 prisoners and 75 guns.

Grand Strategic Plans Evolve

Even as the Aisne-Marne offensive was unfolding, Foch met with Haig and Pershing on July 24 to plan the next moves on the Western Front. The Allies now held the strategic initiative, and all three commanders were determined that they should keep it. They launched a series of powerful offensives in rapid succession to prevent the Germans from reorganizing. The first objective of these drives would be the seizure of three main railroad lines whose possession by the Allies would make future operations easier. The first was the Marne section of the line between

Paris and Verdun, which was already being taken by the Allies in the Aisne-Marne offensive. The second was the line between Paris and Amiens, which a British offensive, scheduled for the Amiens sector on August 8, would open. The third, the section of the line between Paris and Nancy south of Verdun, was to be secured by an American offensive against the St. Mihiel salient. Once these three primary objectives had been secured, the Allies would launch further drives to retake the coal-mining regions of northeastern France, and to drive the right-flank German armies back along the southern coast of the English Channel.

On August 2, Ludendorff revealed his own failing grasp of the situation. Unaware of the Allied plans, he made an assessment that no further Allied offensives should be expected in the immediate future, although in the longer term, the Allies might attack south of Ypres, east of Reims, against the St. Mihiel salient, or in Lorraine. Ludendorff nevertheless decided that Germany must go over to the strategic defensive on the

Paris
For further references
see pages
63, 124

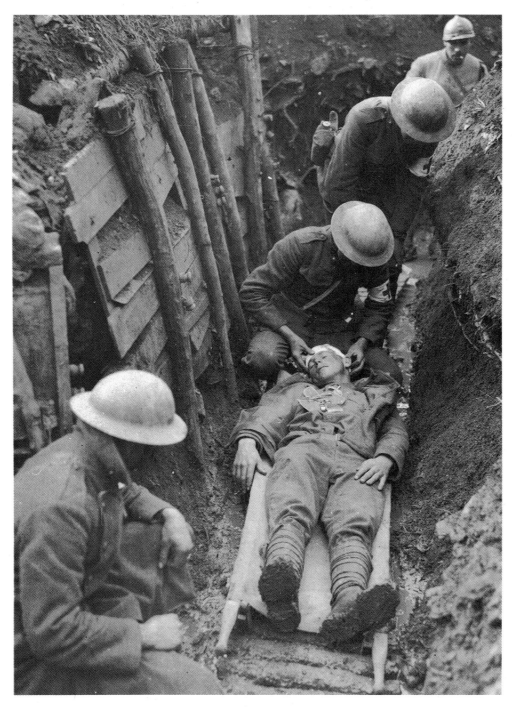

A Marine receives first aid in the trenches of the Toulon Sector in 1918.

Western Front, while he gathered his forces for surprise offensives designed not to take ground, but to inflict casualties on the Allies.

The Creation of an American Army

By August 1918, Pershing thought that his divisions were ready for battle as a unified force under American command. Each of these divisions had a strength of nearly 28,000 men, nearly twice that of the divisions fielded by the exhausted British and French during 1918.

The Allies had finally agreed on April 3 to the appointment of a single commander-in-chief for all the Allied forces in France. The officer selected was the French general, Foch, who had been

General John Joseph Pershing, seen here in a 1919 photograph, ran the American Expeditionary Forces in France during World War I almost as an independent branch of the armed forces, but he had full political support for his determined stand against Allied efforts to integrate American formations into Allied armies.

promoted to marshal after the successful conclusion of the Aisne-Marne offensive. Under pressure from Pershing and his political masters, Foch finally agreed on July 24 that after the return of the dispersed American divisions to Pershing's command, the American Expeditionary Force should form its own independent army and have its own sector of the front.

Pershing had often been characterized as selfish in his determination that the Americans should fight as an American army under American command in an American sector of the line. However, this ignores the fact that Pershing had proved willing to lend his divisions to the British and French during times of crisis, but he steadily opposed the use of American divisions to flesh out depleted British and French corps on a piecemeal basis, which would have left the Americans without a major success of their own at the end of the war. Pershing's willingness to see parts of the A.E.F. under Allied command is proved by the fact that II Corps remained under British command for the rest of the war.

The sole exception to Pershing's basic principle was the 93rd Division, a formation without artillery and essential support trains. The 93rd Division was one of two African-American divisions sent to France during World War I. The regiments of the division were allocated to the French, and after a thorough reorganiza-

1st Lieutenant, 371st Infantry Regiment, U.S. Army, Western Front, France, 1918

The inclusion of black troops in the American Expeditionary Force caused the administration considerable controversy at a time of racial segregation. The A.E.F. included the 92nd Division with four black infantry regiments, and four other regiments (the 369th, 370th, 371st, and 372nd) were sent to France as the components of the intended 93rd Division. Four regiments were allocated to the French army, which had a long tradition of using black troops and used these American regiments to create the 157th Infantry Division "Goybet." The black officers and men of the four regiments wore American uniforms, but for reasons of practicality carried French equipment. This first lieutenant wears an M1917 olive drab tunic. It was based on the M1912 design, but still had four full patch pockets and two collar disks ("US" on the right and the regimental number on the left), the M1912 olive drab semi-breeches with five pockets (two oblique front hip, two rear hip, and right fob), M1917 leather boots, and leather leggings. French equipment includes the M1915 Adrian helmet with a narrow brown leather chinstrap and the ARS gas mask.

tion on French lines, were used within French divisions. The other black formation was the 92nd Division, part of the 1st Army, and thousands more African-Americans were employed in the Services of Supply.

Pershing formally assumed command of the new American 1st Army on August 10. Twenty days later, he assumed responsibility for the sector encompassing the St. Mihiel sector, which lay west of the German fortress city of Metz. At this time, the 1st Army included three formations: the American I and III Corps, totaling 19 divisions, and the French II Colonial Corps.

The Battle of St. Mihiel

A salient is an area that juts into the other side's territory. In 1918, the St. Mihiel salient was a broad-based arrowhead pointing west toward Paris, with the town of St. Mihiel just inside its blunt point. The Germans had created the salient as early as 1914 during one of their first attempts to storm the French fortress area of Verdun, which lies farther down the Meuse River northwest of St. Mihiel. The German attack had been unsuccessful, but at the cost of only 100 men, it had left the German army in possession of this salient. It was 32 miles across at its base and had been a thorn in the side of the French for four years: the salient cut across the main rail line between Paris and Nancy, created problems of communication for the French forces in the area, and made any French plans for an attack into occupied Lorraine impossible. Moreover, the Germans' continued possession of the salient had posed severe problems for the French in the grisly battles for Verdun in 1915-16, and it continued to pose a threat to all Allied activity in the Champagne region.

In July 1918, Pershing had suggested to Foch that the proposed American army should cut its teeth in an offensive to restore the St. Mihiel salient to Allied possession. Foch was initially less than enthusiastic, but Pershing and his staff were convinced that it was the right move. Here

Men of a U.S. machine gun company pass through the ruins of a village flattened by American artillery in the closing stages of the St. Mihiel offensive.

St. Mihiel
For further references see pages
65, 67, 72, *77, 78,* 79

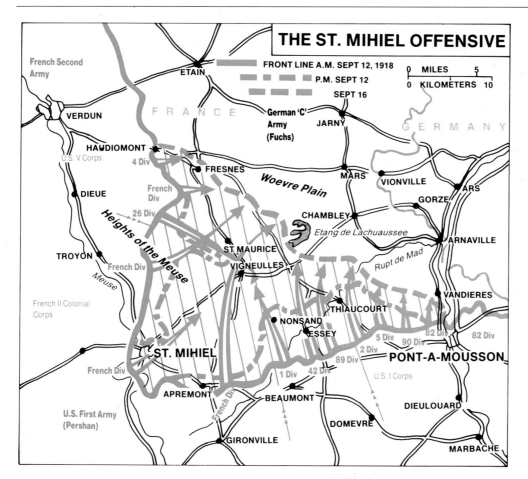

THE ST. MIHIEL OFFENSIVE

FRONT LINE A.M. SEPT 12, 1918

P.M. SEPT 12

SEPT 16

MILES 0 — 5

KILOMETERS 0 — 10

French Second Army

ETAIN

VERDUN

F R A N C E

German 'C' Army (Fuchs)

JARNY

G E R M A N Y

HAUDIOMONT

U.S. V Corps

4 Div

FRESNES

Woevre Plain

MARS

VIONVILLE

ARS

DIEUE

French Div

26 Div

CHAMBLEY

Etang de L'achuaussee

GORZE

ARNAVILLE

Heights of the Meuse

ST MAURICE

TROYON

French Div

VIGNEULLES

Meuse

Rupt de Mad

French II Colonial Corps

VANDIERES

THIAUCOURT

NONSAND

ESSEY

5 Div   90 Div   82 Div   82 Div

ST. MIHIEL

2 Div

89 Div   PONT-A-MOUSSON

French Div

1 Div   42 Div

U.S. I Corps

APREMONT

French Div

BEAUMONT

DIEULOUARD

U.S. First Army (Pershan)

DOMEVRE

GIRONVILLE

MARBACHE

at last was the chance they had long wanted for the American forces to plan and conduct their own offensive on the Western Front. By the time Pershing assumed command of the 1st Army, his staff was already well advanced in planning the American offensive. The original scheme had been to pinch off the salient as far as its base, where the Germans had prepared their so-called *Michel Stellung* (Michael Position), a fortified line held by reserve forces as a fallback line, should the salient be lost. The *Michel Stellung* was made up of two main lines, about three miles apart, at the southern end of the main defensive line known to the Allies as the ''Hindenburg Line.'' But the enthusiasm and confidence of Pershing's staff planners was so great that they soon suggested that the 1st Army's offensive should be on grander lines; as a drive to the northeast reaching the junction of the main east/west and north/south railroad lines behind the base of the salient in the area of Conflans, and then to capture Metz at the juncture of the

Moselle and Seille rivers. Despite the fact that this ambitious concept would involve an attempt to take one of the strongest fortified positions in Europe, it received approval.

The 1st Army's planners decided that the extreme southwestern tip of the salient would be attacked by the II Colonial Corps' four divisions. Their task would be to pin the German forces at their farthest stretch from the *Michel Stellung*. In addition, the 15 divisions that would be committed by the 1st Army's corps (now three in number) would attack and drive in the two faces of the salient. After approving the final plan, Pershing submitted it to Foch.

The Allied commander-in-chief was so enthusiastic that he suggested a major upgrade of the scheme to bring it into line with the grand offensive his own staff was preparing. Foch suggested adding another six French divisions to allow the offensive to be widened by bringing in the French 4th and 8th Armies on the 1st Army's left and right respectively. This

plan would translate Pershing's pinching-off attack into a wide-front general offensive, like those that had cost the British and French so heavily in earlier offensives.

An Effective Compromise Plan

At this point the British commander-in-chief objected. Haig's own strategic vision called for two converging, or pincer, offensives, one in the north along the Somme River via Cambrai toward Aulnoye by British forces and the other in the south by Franco-American forces. As far as Haig was concerned, therefore, the American offensive was about to be launched in the wrong place and in the wrong strategic direction. Haig urged that it would be better to shift the American offensive to the other side of Verdun, where an offensive to the north through the Foret d'Argonne would take Mezieres, a target far easier to capture than Metz. Mezieres was an important road link, and an even more important rail junction on the

routes running behind the German front. It was used by the Germans to shift men and equipment to the most threatened sectors of their line. Its capture by the Allies would be a very heavy blow to the Germans, especially if the British took Aulnoye at much the same time.

Pershing saw that there was much strategic sense in Haig's idea, especially as an American capture of Mezieres would open the chance for his forces to advance down the Meuse to Namur and strike the flank, if not the rear, of the German forces in northern France and Belgium. On August 30, Foch attempted to reconcile the American and British points of view in a scheme of his own. He proposed that the Americans launch only a limited attack against the south face of the St. Mihiel salient, allowing the rest of the 1st Army's strength to be divided between the French 2nd and 4th Armies for an offensive toward Mezieres.

Pershing was all too aware that, while Foch's acceptance of Haig's concept was driven mainly by strategic sense, the

Movement in the conditions of World War I were often difficult. As this photograph of an American ammunition carrier stuck on a road of the St. Mihiel salient shows, one stoppage could completely halt an entire column.

The First World War was an unrelenting war. Sergeant Cy Redlinger of the 1st Infantry Division described his experience in a diary. The year is 1918.

Saturday, August 25. Drill and inspection this morning. The afternoon is ours in which to loaf about. About 2 p.m. sergeants came thru the company streets yelling, "Free tobacco and cigarettes, fall in for free tobacco." So we all fall in and are promptly marched to the R.R. yards to unload a trainload of French machine gun carts. Had to man-handle them out of the cars, then attach the wheels and pull them back to Gondrescourt and line them up in the company street. We were at it until dark and I learned to be wary of any unofficial assemblies.

October 31. Rode in trucks again about five miles. No chow until I p.m. When it finally arrived all we had was coffee, target paste gravy, bacon and bread. Same dose for supper. The road ahead is under artillery fire. Cows mooing in the barn keep us all awake.

November I. Rations came in last night. Foggy this morning. Mail also came in. Got two letters. Heavy artillery fire. Going into the trenches tomorrow.

November 2. Cold and clear. Airplanes active. French observation balloon up this afternoon. Stand to at 5:45. Warmer and starting to rain. Leave at 6 p.m., a four mile hike to our position, packs very heavy. We are slogging thru the mud. Busby and I assigned to a listening post in a clump of bushes in NO MAN's LAND, dark as pitch. Queer shadows and sounds. Have box of grenades. We are both scared. At 10 p.m. three Frenchmen show up. One talks English. We are in the wrong place and they take over; we report to company Hdqrs. where the fourth platoon is in support, in a big dugout. All bunks are occupied. Busby and I sit on packs, backs to the wall and try to sleep.

About 2:30 a.m. a hellish bombardment starts. John Fondron, outside guard comes in covered with mud caused by bursting shells. Wasn't hurt. Barrage lasts fifty minutes. As soon as it lifts, Schussler, company bugler comes in, tells the platoon to report to Co. Hdqrs. Trenches badly caved in, so we go to Co. Hdqrs. on top of trenches. Lots of excitement at Hdqrs. Lt. McLaughlin in a daze. Lt. Erickson comes in with hand bandaged. Hand burned when he lit a flare, calling for French artillery support. Co. Commander orders the fourth platoon to take over the front from the first. I arrive at front line position with Corporal Killen. Homer Givens leaned against post, bleeding from many small wounds, right side from neck to waist. Sturt helping him to rear. He's a big man. Very heavy to drag thru mud filled trenches. Meet four guys with a stretcher and they take him.

Go back to front line, and find Gresham lying dead on the fire step. His feet are in the trench. He is shot in the face and neck. Still warm and limber when Killen and I pick him up. I have him under the arms, Killen has his feet. He is too heavy for us to carry in that position, so I put one of his arms around my neck and around my shoulder. Killen still has his feet and legs. Very foggy morning, so we take him up on top of the trench. The fog hides us from the Boche. We go a short way and meet two other men with a stretcher, so we put him on it and the four of us carry him back to Co. Hdqrs.

November 4. On post with McFarland, Fondron and Sipes last night. Strain eyes looking for Boche. Shoot at any noise or shadows. Long night, very cold. Stay in deep, wet dugout during day, go on post at 4:30 p.m. and stay until daylight.

Allied commander-in-chief also saw in the revision a chance to get the main bulk of the American forces under French command. Foch's new plan called for the use of a smaller 1st Army under Pershing's command, with at least one corps split off for use in a Franco-American army under a French commander. Pershing saw the likelihood later of a renewed French demand that all American forces should be placed under French command. He therefore turned down Haig's plan as developed by Foch. But the American commander did appreciate the merits of Haig's idea and therefore offered to limit his army's offensive, or even to abandon it, on the condition that the 1st Army be left intact.

The compromise solution adopted by the Allied commanders on September 2 resulted in a return to the original concept for the offensive, which would merely pinch off the salient as far to the northeast as the *Michel Stellung*. This would limit the American advance to a line between Pont-a-Mousson in the southeast

to Haudiomont in the northwest, but it would still give the Americans the offensive they wanted so much. It would also gain strategically important territory, but would probably result in relatively few casualties and therefore leave the 1st Army in good shape for an immediate move north to play its part in the Meuse-Argonne operation.

Thus Pershing's staff was faced with the complex task of finalizing the army's arrangements for the forthcoming St. Mihiel battle while planning for the next battle, which was scheduled to start 23 days later and 40 miles away. Nothing so ambitious had previously been attempted by any of the Allied armies in World War I.

The German defense of the St. Mihiel salient included 75,000 men in the eight divisions controlled by three corps of General Lieutenant Fuch's Army Detachment "C" within the German Army Group "Gallwitz." In the final American plan this strength was to be attacked by 264,000 men of the 1st Army (216,000 Americans and 48,000 French). The Germans were

As they pushed into the St. Mihiel salient, American and French forces moved into territory that had been little affected by the physical devastation of the war, as shown in this photograph of the area just ten miles short of St. Mihiel.

Above: The long-range pounding of heavy targets was undertaken by heavy artillery such as this U.S. Navy equipment. Such weapons could use the good railroad network behind the Allied lines in north eastern France to reach any sector where their capabilities were needed.

Right: Gas was a major weapon in the later stages of World War I. This 1918 photograph reveals men of the U.S. Marine Corps responding to a gas alarm in the Verdun sector.

to be pinned at the salient's tip by three divisions of General de Corps d'Armee Blondlat's II Colonial Corps. It was hoped that this frontal assault would hold the Germans long enough for the direct attacks on the salient's western and southern faces to break through and cut the Germans' lines of retreat. On the western face, the attack would be made by three divisions (the 26th ''Yankee'' Division flanked by two French divisions) of Major General George H. Cameron's V Corps; on the southern face, a larger effort would be made by six divisions of Major General Joseph T. Dickman's IV Corps (the 1st, 42nd, and 89th Divisions) and of Major General Liggett's I Corps (the 2nd, 5th, and 90th Divisions). The formations of the 1st Army began to move into position on August 30.

By the standards of the time, the 1st Army was short of artillery. During the crisis of the spring of 1918, the British and French had requested and received from the United States; the rapid delivery of infantry and machinegun units. These formations now formed the bulk of the 1st

Army, with support provided by 3,000 mainly French guns. About 267 Renault FT light tanks were allocated to the offensive: they were also French, though some were manned by American soldiers of the 304th Tank Brigade, commanded by Lieutenant Colonel George S. Patton, Jr.

Massive Air Support

One of the most far sighted features of the American offensive was the size and set-up of the air support force, allocated under a single commander, Colonel William Mitchell. In this largest-yet concentration of air power for a single offensive, 1,500 aircraft were made available, 609 of them flown by Americans and the others by British, French, Italian, and Portuguese airmen. A comprehensive air plan was created, with two-seaters to fly reconnaissance and artillery spotting operations, and single-seaters to provide protection and scour the skies for any German opposition. All aircraft were to support the ground forces wherever and whenever possible.

The U.S. Army had no American-designed tanks available in World War I and used a combination of British and French equipment. This light tank of the 1st Tank Brigade is a Renault FT, a French vehicle armed with a 37-mm gun. It had a turret capable of a 360° traverse, unlike the guns in heavier tanks of British and French design.

Hunter Liggett
For further references see pages
54, 79, 93, 111, 113, *130*

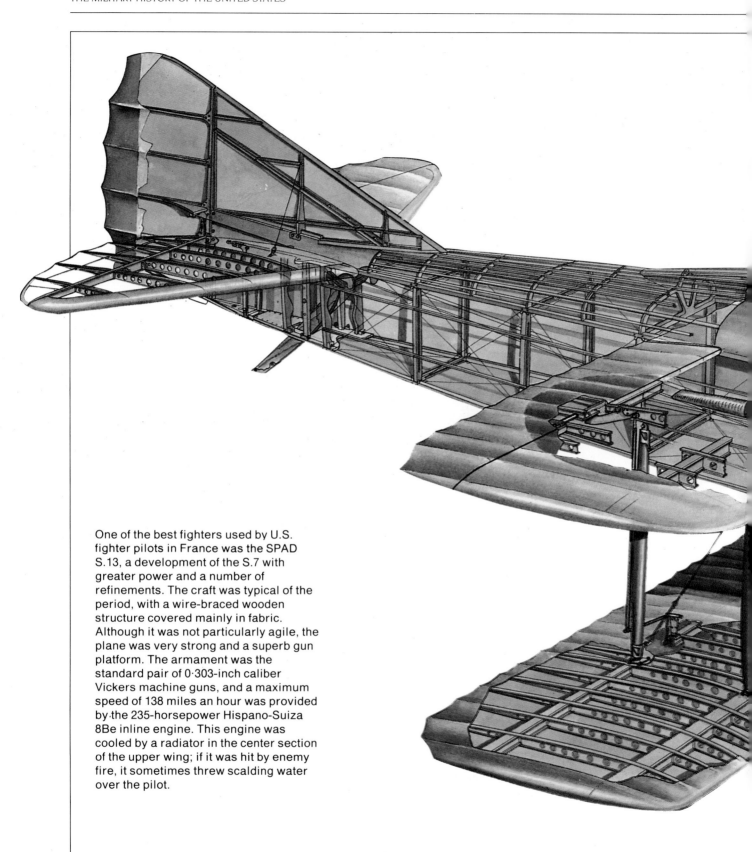

One of the best fighters used by U.S. fighter pilots in France was the SPAD S.13, a development of the S.7 with greater power and a number of refinements. The craft was typical of the period, with a wire-braced wooden structure covered mainly in fabric. Although it was not particularly agile, the plane was very strong and a superb gun platform. The armament was the standard pair of 0·303-inch caliber Vickers machine guns, and a maximum speed of 138 miles an hour was provided by the 235-horsepower Hispano-Suiza 8Be inline engine. This engine was cooled by a radiator in the center section of the upper wing; if it was hit by enemy fire, it sometimes threw scalding water over the pilot.

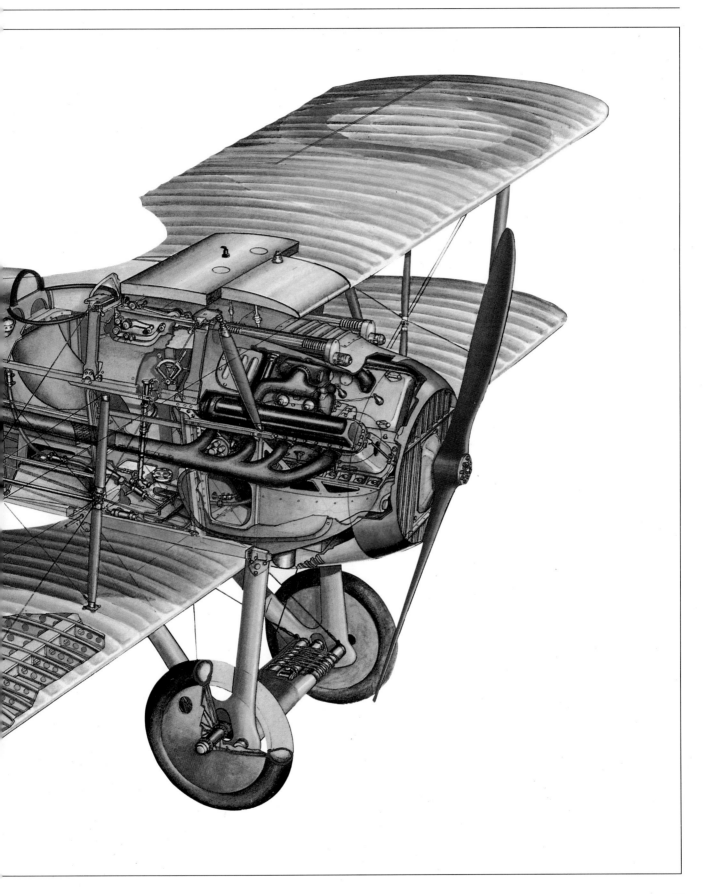

Seen beside a plane carrying his personal insignia is Brigadier General William ''Billy'' Mitchell, the far sighted commander of the U.S. air units in France.

Surprise has always been one of the most decisive factors in war, and the 1st Army went to great lengths in its efforts to dupe the Germans about the location and timing of the offensive. Troops moved into their positions only at night, and artillery was shifted into pre-camouflaged firing sites. None of this fooled the war-wise Germans. European newspapers also headlined the American build-up, and one Swiss newspaper actually predicted the exact location and launch time of the offensive! But the young, eager, and physically tough American soldiers were confident in themselves and in their commanders, and

expected to beat the Germans without difficulty.

The Germans Begin Their Evacuation

On September 8, Ludendorff ordered the evacuation of the St. Mihiel salient, which was only lightly garrisoned. On September 11, the Germans began the wearisome task of removing their heavy artillery and supplies.

Preparations moved to their peak shortly before the offensive's launch date of September 12. On the rain-swept night

Right: A U.S. major in the basket of an observation balloon. The officer's clothing, as well as the neat checkerboard of the fields below, indicates that this photograph was not taken over the front. On the left of the basket is the pack containing the observer's parachute, a static type that opened after the jumper's descent had pulled it out of an outer pack that was anchored to the basket.

One of the major training airfields for American aircrews in France was Issoudun, seen here accommodating a large number of dual-control trainers. These are Nieuport 80-series aircraft based on the obsolete Nieuport 12 two-seat fighter.

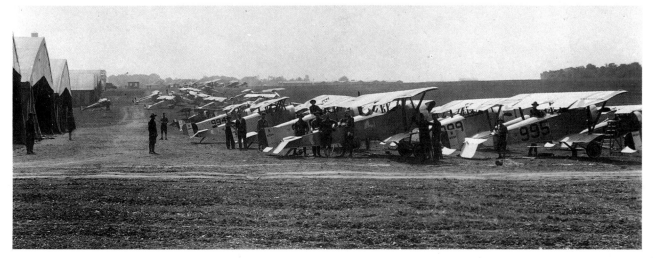

The DH-4, beset by major production problems in the United States, had to be modified to operational standard after it reached France. The type flew its first combat sortie on August 2, 1918, by which time it was obsolescent, for the British original had entered service in 1916. Even so, the DH-4 served with 13 U.S. squadrons in France and remained a mainstay of the later U.S. Army Air Corps until the late 1920s.

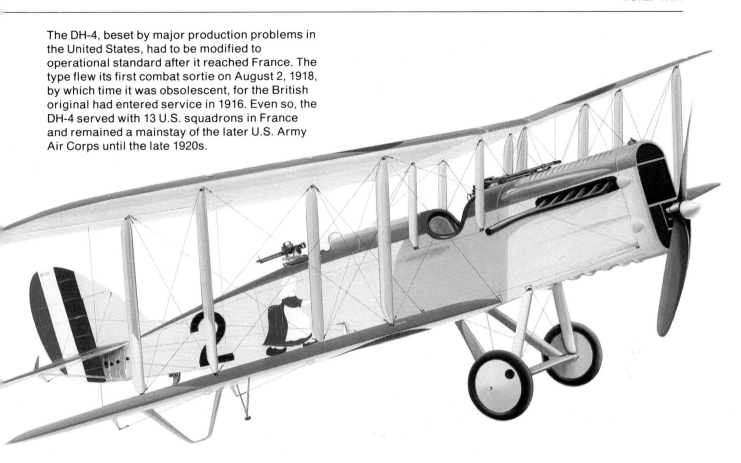

Opposite Top: U.S. craftsmen made propellers that were carved from blanks made of several layers of thin wood laminated together, and were completed to very fine tolerances.

Opposite Below: The wing and fuselage room of the minor repair depot at Issoudun. There were always large numbers of minor accidents needing comparatively small-scale repair at training airfields, and it made logistical sense to carry them out locally.

of September 11-12, the infantry moved up into the front-line trenches. At 1:00 a.m. on September 12, the artillery barrage crashed out. The light guns concentrated on the German front line and its barbed wire entanglements; the medium and heavy guns tackled the German strong points, artillery positions, and rear-area billets; and the heaviest guns concentrated on the rail lines around Metz so that no reinforcements could be rushed into the salient from the city. Over a period of four hours, this bombardment rained down on the Germans, and to the inexperienced American infantry, it appeared that no one and nothing could survive such a hammering. At 5:00 a.m., the bombardment changed character as the range was shortened. This marked the start of the creeping barrage behind which the infantry and their supporting tanks began their advance toward the German trenches.

As soon as they began to approach their first objectives, the Americans began to see the real nature of modern war. The

ground had been torn apart and was still smoking from the detonation of so many shells. In many places, making any progress at all was difficult, and much of the barbed wire was still standing. The French had warned the Americans that this would be the case, and to supplement the standard issue of wire cutters, many men had bought additional supplies at local hardware stores. Others carried rolls of wire netting to throw over standing entanglements. Even this early stage of the advance proved too much for most of the accompanying tanks, and mechanical failures thinned units which had already lost many of their vehicles to the shell-torn terrain.

So the American troops passed through or over the remains of the barbed wire, all the time expecting at least some German survivors to pop out of their dugouts and man the defenses. But when the attackers reached the German trenches, they found no defenders, dead or alive.

Knowing what was about to fall on his

75

A poster urges the American public not to waste food.

Food *is* Ammunition—
Don't waste it.
UNITED STATES FOOD ADMINISTRATION

men, Fuchs had forestalled Ludendorff and activated a plan to shorten his line. As the 1st Army moved up into its assault positions, the men of Army Detachment ''C'' were melting away to the rear, where they manned the incomplete but shorter *Michel Stellung.* Fuchs had slightly miscalculated the American schedule, and as they pushed forward into the areas behind the German lines, the Americans encountered small parties of retreating Germans. Most of the Germans' invaluable artillery had already been pulled back, so the American troops faced few

problems in mopping up these fall-back parties. The occasional German strongpoint presented greater opposition, but the carefully planned air scheme worked well. When the slowly moving artillery was available, fire was called in by the spotter aircraft.

Gradually, the flow of German prisoners being escorted to the rear increased. It was then considerably swelled by the surrender of a complete but thoroughly demoralized Austro-Hungarian formation. The divisions of I and IV Corps had generally reached their first-day objectives by midday. The corps commanders realized the importance of speed if the Germans were to be trapped, and they urged their men to push forward as quickly as possible: by nightfall, most of the second-day objectives had been reached. In the north, the relatively inexperienced 26th Division was having a harder time of it, and only one battalion reached the division's first-day objective on time. Pershing saw the chance of trapping the German XIII Reserve Corps beginning to slip away through the six-mile gap still separating the leading elements of V Corps' 26th Division and IV Corps' 1st Division. He personally phoned his corps commanders to urge all possible speed. Cameron was ordered to get at least one regiment into Vigneulles on the Germans' main line of retreat. Major General Clarence Edwards of the 26th Division entrusted the task to the 102nd Infantry Regiment of his 51st Brigade, adding that he wanted the regiment to reach Vigneulles before any unit of the 1st Division. The 102nd reached the town at 2:15 a.m. on September 13, while the advance guard of the 1st Division arrived in the town at 6:00 a.m. For the rest of September 13, the Americans and their French allies moved northeast toward the *Michel Stellung*; by nightfall, they had reached the base of the salient.

Virtually Total American Success

So the first major American offensive of the war ended, barely 30 hours after it had started. To the average American soldier, and indeed to many American com-

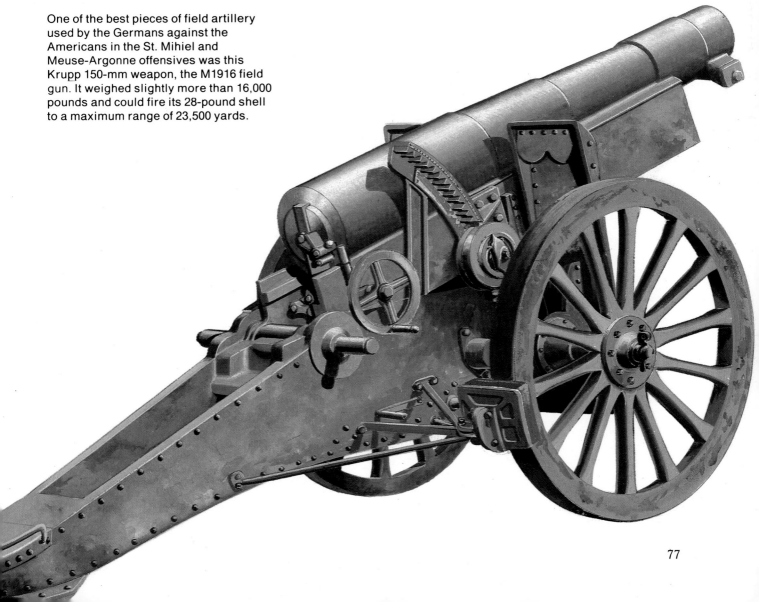

One of the best pieces of field artillery used by the Germans against the Americans in the St. Mihiel and Meuse-Argonne offensives was this Krupp 150-mm weapon, the M1916 field gun. It weighed slightly more than 16,000 pounds and could fire its 28-pound shell to a maximum range of 23,500 yards.

Right: American snipers pick off Germans defenders on the edge of Villers on October 9, 1918. The American forces contained a large number of good marksmen.

Below: German prisoners entertain their American captors after the St. Mihiel offensive.

The wheel turns virtually full circle: the U.S. Marines captured this tank from the Germans, who had captured it from the British, probably after it had become stuck or suffered a mechanical failure.

manders, it seemed a great waste not to press the advantage and assault the *Michel Stellung* itself before advancing toward Metz, but Pershing checked his formations and took stock of the situation. At a cost of 7,000 casualties, the Americans had removed a salient that had troubled the French for four years, capturing 15,000 men and 450 guns in the process. Some critics have tried to play down this first major American success of World War I by referring to "the stroll at St. Mihiel" and "the sector where the Americans relieved the Germans." There is little doubt that the victory was an easy one. But whatever the critics said, it was a victory, and one from which the 1st Army learned a great deal. In addition, the German withdrawal, prompted partly by sensibly shortening the defensive line, was also spurred by a very real dread about what was about to hit them.

Some of the American commanders, notably Pershing and Dickman, wished that the 1st Army might have been allowed to attack the incomplete *Michel Stellung* and advance on Metz. But others, led by Liggett, were probably right in claiming that the 1st Army lacked the skills for such an undertaking. It also lacked the heavy artillery that would have

been needed to make any real impression on the well-prepared defenses of the city. Now American organizational skills were to be tested to the limit: the next task was to move the entire 1st Army some way north in time for the Meuse-Argonne operation.

Planning the Meuse-Argonne Offensive

In some ways, the 1st Army's offensive to eliminate the St. Mihiel salient had been fought in a vacuum. In its final form, the offensive was planned to allow the American soldiers to cut their operational teeth in a limited operation that could still yield useful results. The rest of the Western Front was relatively quiet during the period of the St. Mihiel offensive. The Allied commanders were busy preparing the next stage of their grand offensive, planned by Foch to gain Allied advances deep into Germany before the end of 1918.

The original concept had been for two separate but coordinated offensives. First, British forces would strike east between the upper reaches of the Scarpe and Somme rivers in the northern part of

U.S. soldiers fire a French made Chauchat light machine gun during the offensive at St. Mihiel. This gun was not liked by the troops as the open-sided magazine allowed dirt into the mechanism, jamming it.

the Western Front between Lens and Peronne; at the same time, Franco-American forces would attack northeast in the central sector between Reims and Verdun. Success in both efforts would leave the German armies of Army Group ''Boehn'' in a vulnerable salient between the Oise and Aisne rivers with its tip between Laon and Craonne. The objects of the two offensives were Aulnoye and Mezieres, both key points on the north/south rail line used by the Germans to move reinforcements and supplies between different sectors of the front.

Even in this initial form, the Allied offensives could have yielded great gains, but Foch steadily improved and expanded the basic notion into a grand assault along the entire Western Front as far south as Verdun - ''Tout le monde a la bataille!'' (Everyone into the battle!). The two original offensive thrusts remained, and two more were added: a Franco-British-Belgian offensive in Flanders along the Lys River to the north of Lens, and a Franco-British offensive in the center between Peronne and Reims to link the two main thrusts. Foch's overall plan was based on the knowledge that Germany made effective use of the railroad network in the rear of its armies for supply and reinforcement in offensive opera-

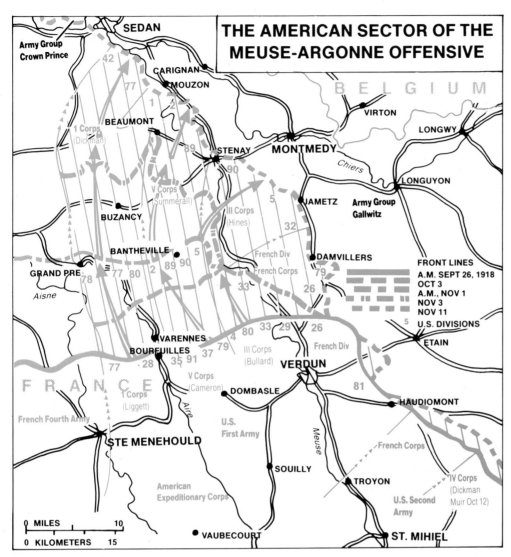

THE AMERICAN SECTOR OF THE MEUSE-ARGONNE OFFENSIVE

The American sector of the Meuse-Argonne offensive, 1918

tions, and for the lateral and rearward movement of men and equipment in defensive operations. The main lateral railroad line, from Bruges in the north to Strasbourg in the south, was fed from the east by lines running from Germany's industrial and population centers in the Rhine River valley and moved men and equipment west to the Western Front. The main junctions on this lateral railroad line were vital to Germany's continued war effort in the west; the most important were Aulnoye, Maubeuge, Longuyon, and Mezieres.

Germany's Strategic Plan

This situation was seen just as clearly by Ludendorff, who saw Germany's only hope as a withdrawal to shorter lines that could be defended more easily with less manpower and materiel. He intended to implement this withdrawal only when Allied pressure made it necessary, and would study it with delaying battles to hold the Allies and inflict maximum casualties on them. Ludendorff's plan depended on the river and canal lines as well as a number of fortified positions. He felt that his major problem was the movement of German forces from Flanders and the great westward bulge of the Western Front around Laon. Some of the senior field commanders on the Western Front advocated a rapid withdrawal to a line between Antwerp and the Meuse River, but Ludendorff refused to consider it since it would inevitably mean the losing of irreplaceable equip-

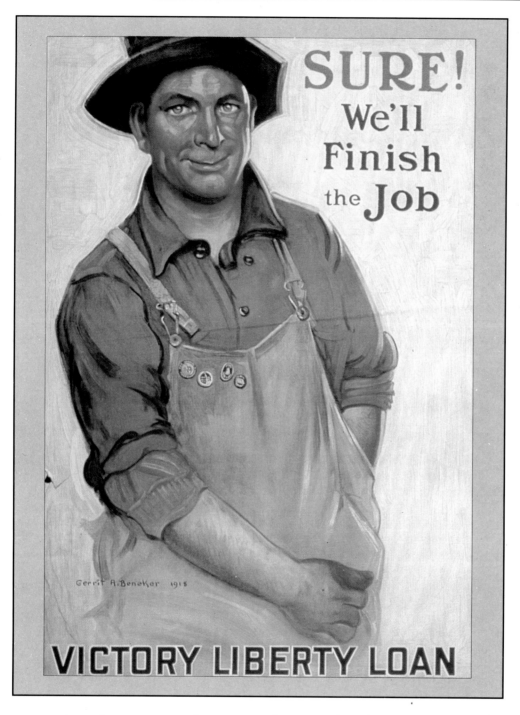

SURE!
We'll
Finish
the Job

Gerrit A.Beneker 1918

VICTORY LIBERTY LOAN

It was not just with work that the American public supported the war effort, but also with loans that paid for the vast military and industrial machine that had sprung into existence.

ment and supplies on a vast scale.

In all, Foch's grand offensive would involve 220 Allied divisions (160 in the line and 60 in reserve), including 42 powerful American divisions. Of the American divisions, ten were allocated to British and French armies, leaving 32 at Pershing's immediate disposal. Some of the American formations had just arrived, so they had less battle value, and a shortage of replacements meant that Pershing needed to cannibalize some units to bring his front-line formations up to strength.

Within this much enlared scheme, the Franco-American drive on the right scheduled to start the earliest, had three main strategic objectives. It was designed to recapture French territory occupied by the Germans since the opening weeks of

the war, to take the communications center at Mezieres to hinder the Germans' ability to shift forces left and right across their front, and to drive the Germans across the Meuse River between Sedan and Mezieres before pinning them against the forested hills of the Ardennes. The Allied high command assumed that the Ardennes region was impassable, and that therefore the Germans would not be able to extricate themselves from an envelopment on three exposed sides.

Planning and preparation for so grand an offensive could not be concealed completely, and the Germans were aware in general terms of what was about to fall on them. They were certainly demoralized by recent reverses, the epidemic of devastating influenza that had swept the army, lack of adequate reinforcements, and the distressing news of increasing hunger at home. On the other hand, the Germans were immensely skilled in the difficult art of defensive fighting. Sometimes commanders would opt for an elastic defense, firm in some places, but yield-

ing in others. The tactic would induce attackers into hasty local advances that could then be nipped off by local counterattacks before the Germans launched a counteroffensive. Sometimes they would choose a defense centered on layers of strong points to persuade the attackers to sidestep major obstacles in an effort to maintain the momentum of their offensive. This would give the defenders the chance to strike at the attackers' flanks and rear once the leading elements had passed by. Sometimes they would use a mixture of both these concepts.

The Formidable Argonne

The sector allocated to the 1st Army for its offensive was the Argonne. This region is bounded to the east and west by the valleys of the Meuse and Aisne rivers, which are separated by a broken ridge line. There are commanding heights at Montfaucon, Romagne, Cunel, and Barricourt; in the east are the Heights of the

Photographed on September 18, 1918, these recuperating American officers play cards with Mrs. W.E. Covey at the Covey Home for Convalescent Officers at Chateau de Villagenis at Plalaiseau.

The segregation of the period meant that black soldiers were entertained at places like this club opened by African-American women in 1918.

Meuse and in the west, the Foret d'Argonne (Argonne Forest).

This area had been in German hands for four years, giving local commanders all the time they needed to prepare their defenses to an overall depth of 12 miles with a real maze of barbed wire entanglements, machine-gun nests, and mutually supporting strong points. The forward defensive line was a northward extension of the *Michel Stellung* and lay about two miles behind the German front line. It was moderately strong in any case, but its main purpose was to serve as a trip-wire for the fully fledged defensive position about six miles behind the *Michel Stellung*, which included two more lines about two miles apart. The forward line was the *Kriemhilde Stellung* (Kriemhilde Position) and the rear line the *Brunhilde und Freya Stellungen* (Brunhilde and Freya Positions). The sector assigned to the 1st Army lay on the junction between two German armies belonging to General Max von Gallwitz's German 5th Army of Army Group "Gallwitz" in the east and Generaloberst Karl von Einem's German

3rd Army of Army Group "Kronprinz Wilhelm" in the west. The forward line, the *Michel Stellung*, ran through both armies, while the intermediate line, the *Kriemhilde Stellung*, passed through the 5th Army. The rear line, common to both armies, was designated the *Freya Stellung* in the 5th Army's sector and the *Brunhilde Stellung* in the 3rd Army's sector. The 5th Army had seven divisions in the line with three more in reserve, while the 3rd Army mustered ten divisions in the line with four in reserve.

Each line made the best possible use of the natural defensive features provided by the terrain. They consisted of trenches protected by barbed wire, machine-gun nests, and concrete fighting posts. Local strengthening was provided by clusters of strong points, the most formidable at Montfaucon, Cunel, and Barricourt.

Work had been started on a fourth defensive line running parallel to the *Brunhilde und Freya Stellungen* about four miles further to the rear between Buzancy and Dun, but the Germans had achieved little more than basic surveying

Above: U.S. gunners ram home the 14-inch projectile of a heavy rail gun behind the Argonne front. The metal projectile was followed into the breech by a varying number of bagged propellant charges, with the full load providing a maximum range of 20 miles or more.

and limited preparation of the ground.

These defense lines were greatly aided in the west by the nature of the Foret d'Argonne between the Aisne and Aire Rivers, and the Bois de Cheppy (Cheppy Wood) east of the Aire River. The Foret d'Argonne, and to a lesser extent the Bois de Cheppy, consisted of dense timber on extremely uneven ground. Deep ravines made movement extremely difficult. The

Right: U.S. Marines move up a shattered hill during the Argonne offensive. Such men were fully aware that such devastation did not necessarily mean that the defenders had all been killed, hence the caution with which the men are moving.

Germans had helped nature, for in the previous four years they had filled the forest and the woods with wire entanglements that were secure even against tanks because of the uneven forest floor and the close spacing of the trees. In addition, the American troops found to their cost all that could be achieved by standard artillery bombardment was to convert standing timber into a mass of fallen and sharply splintered wood that just added to the barrier created by the wire.

The Germans Exploit Nature

The land east of the Aire River was more open but, on the right flank of the American sector, it was split by the Meuse River. This major waterway flowed north through Verdun toward Sedan, which was the farthest that the Americans were scheduled to advance. The Meuse River and the bluffs on each side of it

(especially the Heights of the Meuse on the west) were in themselves formidable natural obstacles. In addition, the Germans had turned the whole area into a desert as part of a deliberate "scorched earth" policy. Towns and villages had been burned; road and rail bridges had been demolished, cuts and embankments had been destroyed with explosives; wells and other sources of water had been polluted; and the whole area had been littered with booby traps. When their advance reached this area, therefore, the American troops had to move with great caution. They were forced to bring up all their water and food, and to watch out for everything that might be booby-trapped. The result was a small but demoralizing stream of American casualties and a slowing of the offensive momentum. Any advance was also hindered by the fact that there were only two usable roads in the region. They lay toward each flank, and any movement on them resulted in a

American cameramen film artillery action in the course of the Argonne offensive. Such movies were rushed back to the United States and helped to bring home to the American public the nature of the war in Europe.

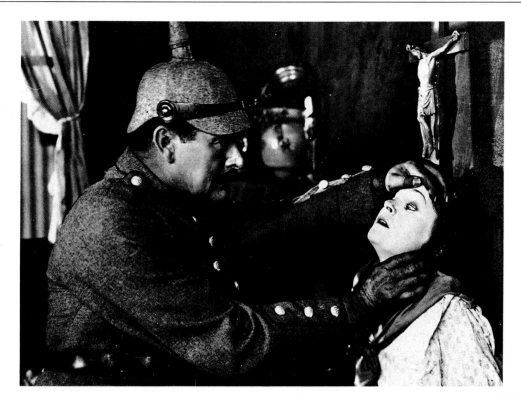

Left: Another way in which the anger of the American public was kept high against the Germans was the "faction" movie supposedly based on true stories. This still from a "Liberty Loan" fund-raising movie called *Stake Uncle Sam to Play Your Hand* starred Mae Marsh as a Belgian girl suffering the attentions of A.C. Gibbons as a German soldier.

Below: U.S. trooops in a French Renault tank in the Argonne forest.

deluge of German artillery fire controlled by observation posts on all available high ground.

Many of these defensive measures were discovered by aerial reconnaissance as the 1st Army began to move into the sector. The sector had been relatively quiet for some time: the total movement of 800,000 men involved the departure of only 200,000 Frenchmen to make room for 600,000 Americans along a 22-mile length of front. On the 1st Army's left was General H. J. E. Gouraud's French 4th Army, the American forces' partner in the offensive. The logistical problem associated with the movement of so many men with all their equipment and supplies was enormous. Road and rail links scarcely existed, and great credit must go to one of Pershing's staff, Colonel George C. Marshall. This officer planned and coordinated the vast move with an impressively capable hand, and the relocation was achieved in the remarkably short time of ten days.

Allied Support for the Americans

The American troops again lacked the heavier equipment so important to

U.S. machine gunners northeast of Villers Tournville, May 1918.

modern warfare. Once more, the Allies met the need: most of the 2,700 guns (and almost all of the heavy artillery) were supplied by the British and French, all 190 Renault FT light tanks were furnished by the French, and Anglo-French efforts boosted the number of available aircraft to 800.

The whole undertaking was one of daunting difficulty. Their success at St. Mihiel had persuaded many ordinary soldiers that they were more than a match for the Germans, but their senior officers did not share this impression. They were all too aware that the offensive had been something of an oddity by the standards of this war, and that it had been fought as much for political as military reasons. Certainly a number of useful military lessons had been learned by the divisions involved, but the commanders were on their guard against any sense of complacency after a victory against forces conducting a planned and orderly withdrawal.

Pershing was fully aware of the difficulties faced by his army in the Meuse-Argonne offensive. He also knew that, if the Allies were to achieve the decisive step of pushing the Germans back behind their own frontier before the end of 1918, his army had to succeed. Any failure now would inevitably delay an Allied victory by six months. As Pershing knew, the offensive was vital to Allied plans, and he appreciated that his relatively

Left: The exploding fragments from an incendiary phosphorus bomb silhouette a U.S. soldier during a night attack on September 21, 1918.

Below: Mobile antiaircraft searchlights of the Corps of Engineers. Such lights could both dazzle aircrews causing pilots to lose control of their aircraft, and illuminate the aircraft for engagement by antiaircraft guns.

U.S. Marine Corps
mechanics with a
Curtiss R-6 floatplane,
a type used mainly for
coastal
reconnaissance
against German
submarines.

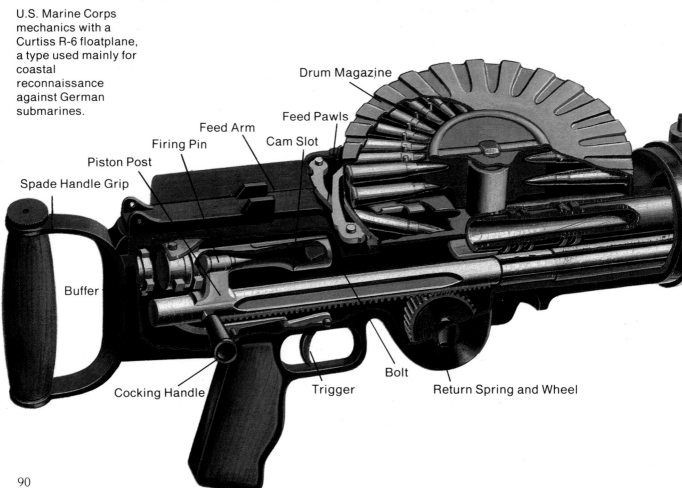

Drum Magazine

Feed Pawls

Feed Arm

Cam Slot

Firing Pin

Piston Post

Spade Handle Grip

Buffer

Cocking Handle

Trigger

Bolt

Return Spring and Wheel

Supported on a tripod for the sustained-fire role, the M1917 was the first of the classic machine guns designed by John Moses Browning. This water-cooled and gas-operated weapon fired its 0.3-inch bullets with a muzzle velocity of 2,800 feet per second. The type had a cyclic rate of between 450 and 600 rounds a minute, and during World War I it was fed by a 250-round fabric belt.

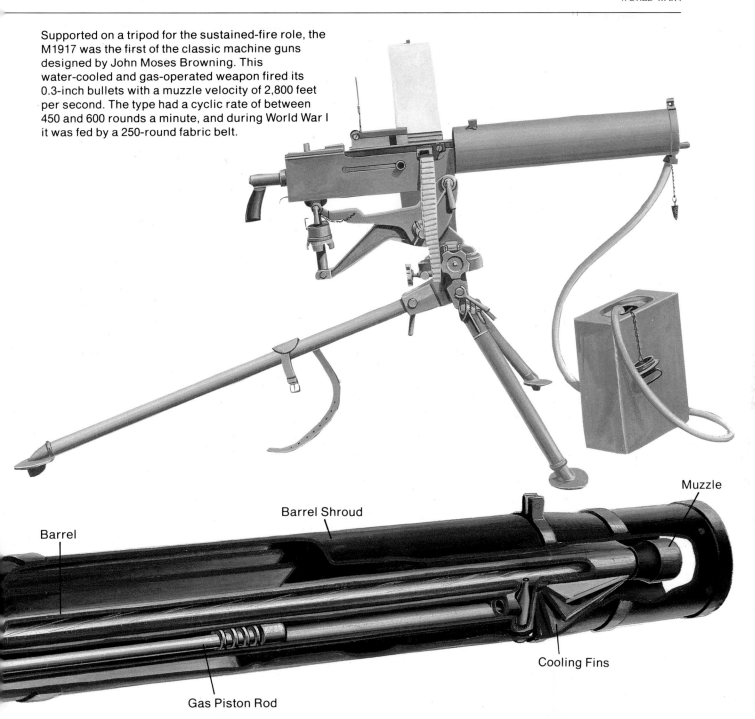

Barrel

Barrel Shroud

Muzzle

Gas Piston Rod

Cooling Fins

In addition to 1,050 weapons in 0·303-inch caliber procured for training, the U.S. government bought the 0·3-inch caliber version of the Lewis light machine gun for operational use. The 2,500 ground-based weapons were used only by the Navy and Marine Corps, while 39,200 were procured for use as trainable guns on American aircraft. This is a ground-based weapon with its full cooling jacket. The Lewis was an air-cooled, gas-operated weapon, which weighed 26 pounds complete with its firing bipod. The weapon was 50·5 inches long and was fed from the overhead drum containing 47 rounds.

green divisions would probably suffer heavy casualties. He also realized that a delay would condemn his forces to spending the winter in their lines west of Verdun. There, they would be victims of German artillery bombardments and prey to the full range of diseases that had already cost the other Allies so dearly in previous winters. In addition to these losses, Pershing knew he would then have higher battle casualties if the German forces had the winter in which to complete their defensive arrangements. Another factor that he had to take into account, but which was more difficult to assess, was the morale of the

Top: U.S. troops on their way to the front in July 1918 are seen passing through Meaux.

Above: Most of the heavy artillery used by U.S. forces in World War I was of French origin. This 155-mm gun is typical.

Opposite Bottom: "Doughboys" relax with female volunteers of the army support organization that achieved full legal military status in 1943 as the Women's Army Corps.

American soldiers. In September 1918, the American divisions were often green, but they were highly enthusiastic. After a winter in the trenches they might be more competent in purely military terms, but their enthusiasm would have been dulled.

The American Deployment

The Meuse-Argonne drive was the first element of the Allies' grand offensive, and it was scheduled to start on September 26. Pershing had at the disposal of his 1st Army one cavalry and 15 infantry divisions divided among three corps. The commander decided to dispose his corps in line abreast for a simultaneous advance with a possible nine divisions. The remaining seven divisions would be held back, three in immediate reserve and the other four, including the cavalry division, in army reserve.

On the left, Liggett's I Corps deployed the 77th, 28th, and 35th Divisions against the right wing of the German 3rd Army's Gardekommando 58. In the center, Cameron's V Corps deployed the 91st,

37th, and 79th Divisions against the left wing of Gardekommando 58. On the right, Bullard's III Corps deployed the 4th, 80th, and 33rd Divisions against the German 5th Army's XXI Corps, with the 29th, 26th, and 8th Divisions occupying the corps' eastern and southeastern front to the point that it linked with the French XVII Corps. These right-flank formations faced the German 5th Army's V Reserve Corps and XVIII Corps on the right bank of the Meuse River. In this last area, no advance was planned. Pershing thus ignored the fact that this would leave the Germans on the Heights of the Meuse. From there, they could watch the progress of the American offensive to the west and call down artillery fire as necessary.

The plan of attack supposed an eight-to-one manpower superiority over the Germans, and Pershing called for each of his corps to commit two divisions forward with the third in reserve. Behind them, the immediate reserves were the 92nd, 32nd, and 3rd Divisions, allocated to the I, V, and III Corps. The army reserve was composed of the 1st, 2nd, and 42nd Divisions,

Seaman 1st Class, U.S. Navy, North Atlantic, 1918

The U.S. Navy was heavily involved in convoy escort work on the North Atlantic route. One of its battle squadrons also served with the British Grand Fleet in blockading Germany's North Sea ports and tempting the German High Seas Fleet into a decisive battle. This seaman wears the standard naval uniform of the period with the distinctive cap and triple stripes on the cuffs and collar.

An American ambulance comes to grief on a slippery French road during October 1918.

plus the cavalry division. Given his superiority in men, Pershing hoped to break through the full eight to ten miles of the German defensive zone in a single concentrated drive within a period of 24 hours. He knew, however, that the Germans had other plans, and that the inexperience of his formations made such hopes risky.

Pershing's Plan

Pershing's plan fell into three main phases. In the first, the 1st Army and the French 4th Army would advance on each side of the Foret d'Argonne to meet at Grandpre. In the second, the two armies would press ahead to the line between La Chesne and Stenay, outflanking the German positions east of the Aisne River and paving the way for the planned Franco-American advance to Sedan and

Mezieres. In the third, the 1st Army would capture the Heights of the Meuse.

Within this overall scheme, the 1st Army's part in the first phase was a swift penetration in massive strength to take the heights at Montfaucon, Romagne, and Cunel.

The date for the launch of the offensive was set by the schedule for the Allies' grand offensive, and it imposed severe strains on the fledgling logistic apparatus of the 1st Army. The necessary American divisions did arrive from the St. Mihiel sector in time for -the Meuse-Argonne offensive, but generally not in shape or time for use in the initial assault. Among the front-line divisions, the only formations with adequate battle experience were therefore the 28th Division of I Corps and the 4th Division of III Corps. This meant that I and III Corps were both attacking with two inexperienced forma-

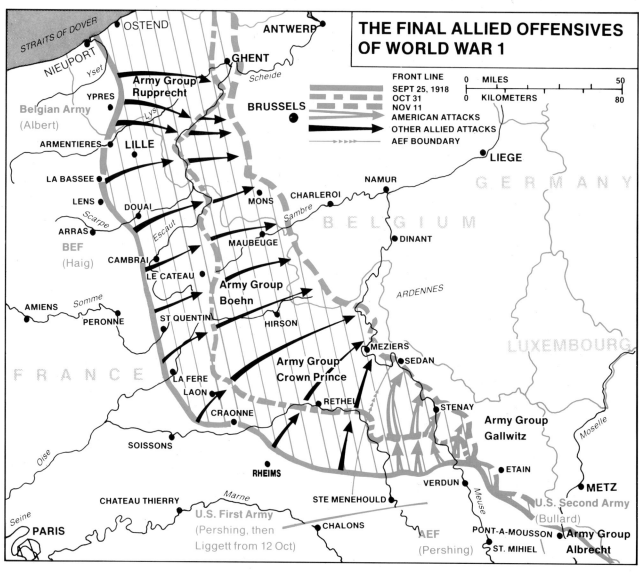

THE FINAL ALLIED OFFENSIVES OF WORLD WAR 1

FRONT LINE
SEPT 25, 1918
OCT 31
NOV 11
AMERICAN ATTACKS
OTHER ALLIED ATTACKS
AEF BOUNDARY

0 MILES 50
0 KILOMETERS 80

STRAITS OF DOVER
OSTEND
ANTWERP
NIEUPORT
Yset
GHENT
Scheide
Army Group Rupprecht
YPRES
BRUSSELS
Belgian Army (Albert)
Lys
LIEGE
ARMENTIERES
LILLE
NAMUR
GERMANY
LA BASSEE
CHARLEROI
LENS
DOUAI
MONS
Sambre
BELGIUM
Scarpe
ARRAS
Escaut
MAUBEUGE
DINANT
BEF (Haig)
CAMBRAI
LE CATEAU
AMIENS
Somme
Army Group Boehn
ARDENNES
PERONNE
ST QUENTIN
HIRSON
FRANCE
MEZIERS
LUXEMBOURG
SEDAN
Army Group Crown Prince
LA FERE
LAON
RETHEL
STENAY
CRAONNE
Moselle
Army Group Gallwitz
SOISSONS
Oise
ETAIN
RHEIMS
STE MENEHOULD
VERDUN
METZ
Marne
CHATEAU THIERRY
U.S. Second Army (Bullard)
Seine
PARIS
U.S. First Army (Pershing, then Liggett from 12 Oct)
CHALONS
AEF (Pershing)
Meuse
PONT-A-MOUSSON
ST. MIHIEL
Army Group Albrecht

The final Allied offensives.

tions, and V Corps with three green formations. The veteran divisions available to the 1st Army, notably the 1st, 2nd, and 42nd Divisions, were resting in the rear area. After a few days, they would be available to move into the line and replace any green division that had got into difficulty.

On the other side of the line, the Germans' forward positions opposite the 1st Army were manned by five divisions, of which four were officially classified as low grade. This gave the American forces the eight-to-one infantry superiority they thought adequate, but their numerical superiority gave a somewhat false impression. One infantryman in a rifle-pit could easily pick off eight infantrymen advancing across open ground, and the im-

balance in favor of the defense increased where there was difficult terrain. Wooded areas such as the Foret d'Argonne offered the possibility of well-concealed defensive positions from which to pick off inexperienced attackers as they called to their comrades in an effort to keep up with each other as they moved forward.

The final American strength in the sector was 630,000 men, and in an effort to halt the formations fleshed out by these men, the Germans eventually committed no fewer than 40 divisions to the region. Ludendorff, who was effectively the German commander-in-chief in his capacity as deputy to General-feldmarschall Paul von Hindenburg and quartermaster general of the German army, believed in strategic withdrawal where necessary. In the Meuse-Argonne region, however, Ludendorff felt that withdrawal would become a scarcely controlled retreat, which would provide a great boost to Allied morale. Ludendorff stuck strongly to the idea that the only sensible course for the Germans was to check the Allies' most powerful armies throughout the winter of 1918-19. In the process, they should inflict losses so heavy that the Allies would welcome a negotiated settlement instead of pressing on with spring offensives that would cost them so many men against a revived German army.

The Meuse-Argonne Offensive

The Meuse-Argonne offensive fell into three main phases. The first lasted from September 26 to October 3, when the American offensive lost its initial momentum in face of increasingly severe German resistance and the exhaustion of the first-line divisions. The second lasted from October 4 to the end of the month. It was marked by a relative lull in the offensive as the initial first-line divisions

Above: The highest-scoring American ace of World War I was Captain Edward V. Rickenbacker with 26 aerial victories.

Left: A pre-war racing driver, Rickenbacker flew with the 94th "Hat in Ring" Aero Squadron. He was awarded the Medal of Honor and the Distinguished Service Cross, as well as two French decorations.

U.S. soldiers rest, if only temporarily, in a German trench captured during the Argonne offensive.

were replaced by more experienced formations brought up from reserve to fight a set-piece campaign against the Germans. The third and final stage, which lasted from November 1 to the Armistice of November 11, was marked by a successful recapture of the campaign's first momentum and some spectacular gains as the 1st Army moved steadily forward to the Meuse River between Sedan and Stenay.

The preliminary bombardment by 2,700 pieces of artillery crashed out at 2:30 in the morning of September 26, saturating the German forward positions, rear areas, and artillery lines with a hail of shells of all calibers. As always in such World War I bombardments, it appeared that no one and nothing could survive the welter of explosive and steel fragments - and as always, the damage was far less than it

first seemed, failing to cut all the wire entanglements and allowing defenders to storm out of their dugouts to man their machine guns as the attackers approached.

The bombardment lasted three hours. In its later stages, it switched into a shorter-range cannonade that became the creeping barrage behind which the first-line units were to advance. At 5:30 a.m., five minutes later than the French 4th Army and just before daylight on a day of cold wind and steady rain, the leading waves of American infantry rose from their forward trenches and moved against the Germans. Some of the front-line divisions had been in position long enough to have reconnoitered the ground in front of them, but others had arrived during the night and had to advance in almost complete ignorance of the terrain, except where divisional intelligence had been able to supply some details.

Abysmal Weather Conditions

The weather was bad for the entire first day and remained dismal for much of the time up to the end of the war. American forces were in action for 47 days between the beginning of the Meuse-Argonne offensive and the Armistice; it rained on 40 of those days. Wet clothes were a constant source of irritation, and the patter of raindrops on steel helmets seemed always to cause increasingly severe headaches. These seemingly small matters came to dominate the feelings of many soldiers in the closing stages of the war. Just as bad was the anger felt at the problems caused by an over-extended supply network forced to operate on too few roads. Tracks turned into mudslides and slowed progress dramatically, but as far as the average soldier was concerned, the worst difficulty was getting food.

The American assault took the Germans by tactical surprise. German commanders in the sector had, of course, expected a Franco-American advance, but were caught completely off guard by the speed with which the Americans had been able to move their 1st Army from the St. Mihiel sector. Pershing had hoped for a 10-mile advance in the first 24 hours of the offensive, but the troops managed to push forward only two or three miles. Even this limited success was won, as an

American soldiers near the Meuse River make use of a camouflaged position abandoned by the retreating Germans.

eminent historian of the period has put it, "only as a result of their enormous numerical superiority, their youth and the luck which accompanies it, and their limitless courage, based as it was upon a massive ignorance of the dangers they faced."

On the right, III Corps pushed forward about three miles through the defenses of the *Michel Stellung*. In the center, V Corps achieved similar progress, only to become stalled in front of the strongpoints around Montfaucon. As expected, the smallest advance occurred on the left, where I Corps encountered the grim Foret d'Argonne and managed to gain only about one mile. During the next few days, the hard-pressed infantry pushed forward slowly and did achieve some successes. On September 27, for example, the German positions around Montfaucon fell to an American pincer attack though

it appears that this enveloping movement was something of an accident. The supporting tanks again succumbed to mechanical problems and the muddy conditions, while the general inexperience of the American planners in logistical matters meant that artillery was moved up too slowly to provide the soaked and increasingly exhausted infantry with adequate supporting fire. Congestion and the abysmal state of the roads made the resupply of forward formations all but impossible, and the problem was made far worse by the inexperience of several of the divisions involved. Some commanders failed to live up to expectations, messages were lost or misdirected, units were moved to the wrong areas: in short, there was every chance that the cohesion of the whole offensive might break down. Yet there was progress, the best being

This machine-gun position was adapted from a small shell crater during the Meuse-Argonne offensive.

U.S. soldiers train with their French 37-mm trench howitzer in a second-line position before moving up to the front line. The photograph was taken on September 21, 1918.

that of III Corps on the right and V Corps in the center. But as the leading divisions of the two corps advanced, they came increasingly under fire on their right from German artillery on the Heights of the Meuse and on their left from guns and even machine guns on the outskirts of the Foret d'Argonne. Here, I Corps was still having a very difficult time, leaving the German defenders in a position to rake the left flank of V Corps' advance past the eastern side of the forest.

The weather and supply conditions that made life difficult for III and V Corps also affected I Corps. But in addition, the sodden ravines, dismembered trees and tangled wire of the Foret d'Argonne made military life all but impossible. It is a savage indication of the severity of the fighting that, by September 28, the day on

which Pershing had hoped the whole Foret d'Argonne would be in American hands, less than half of the forest had actually been captured. In the process, I Corps' right-hand formation, the inexperienced 35th Division, had suffered 8,000 casualties and had to be replaced by the experienced 1st Division as the troops settled down to a slogging match to win the rest of the forest.

The other Allied offensives had started soon after the Meuse-Argonne operation. With the exception of the British effort in the Somme sector (aided by the American 27th and 30th Divisions), none made any significant progress at first. But during the first three days of the Allied grand offensive, the German high command saw even these limited successes as a clear indication of what was to come. Luden-

This field hospital was quickly established in a ruined church at Neuvilly in the Foret d'Argonne.

dorff was so dispirited on September 28 that he called on von Hindenburg, and Germany's two most important commanders agreed that the situation was now worse than it had been on August 8. On that "black day of the German army," the British had scored a major success in the Battle of Amiens, the first stage of the vast offensive to the east that was intended to take allied forces to, and then through, the German "Hindenburg Line" defenses. This successful battle, fought with great strength, determination, and skill, crushed the hopes of von Hindenburg and Ludendorff, and the two German commanders called on the Kaiser to end the war. Now the two commanders were even more pessimistic. They felt that Germany would now have to abandon all her military gains in World War I and try to secure peace on the basis of President Wilson's "Fourteen Points." In an address to Congress on January 18, 1918,

Wilson had outlined his "only possible program" for peace. This platform consisted of 14 major items that almost immediately became known as the "Fourteen Points."

They were the following:

1. Open covenants (agreements) reached openly.
2. Freedom of the seas in war and peace.
3. Removal of all trade barriers.
4. Reduction in the scale of national armaments.
5. Impartial adjustment of colonial claims.
6. German and Austro-Hungarian evacuation of all Russian territory and the independent solution by Russia of her own national policy and political development.
7. German evacuation and restoration of Belgium.

8. German evacuation and restoration of all occupied French territory and the return to France of Alsace-Lorraine.
9. Adjustment of Italy's frontiers in line with the desires of national groupings.
10. Independence for the peoples of the Austro-Hungarian empire.
11. The German and Austro-Hungarian evacuation of Rumania, Serbia, and Montenegro, the restoration of occupied territories, and the provision of Serbian access to the Adriatic Sea.
12. The Turkish portions of the Ottoman Empire to be assured secure sovereignty over themselves, but other nationalities within the Ottoman Empire to be granted independence.
13. Independence for Poland, including all areas with a predominantly Polish population, and free Polish access to the Baltic Sea.
14. The establishment of an association of nations to guarantee the liberty and the territorial integrity of all nations great and small.

The "Fourteen Points" were in many ways far sighted, but their emphasis on various kinds of unfettered liberty were not well received with the Allies, let alone the Central Powers. In many European capitals, the "Fourteen Points" were soon cited as clear evidence of the simplistic – and indeed naive – approach of the United States and her president to international politics. Despite the deteriorating war situation that had prompted von Hindenburg and Luden-

First aid for a soldier wounded in the Meuse-Argonne fighting.

Captain, Air Service, U.S. Army, France, 1918

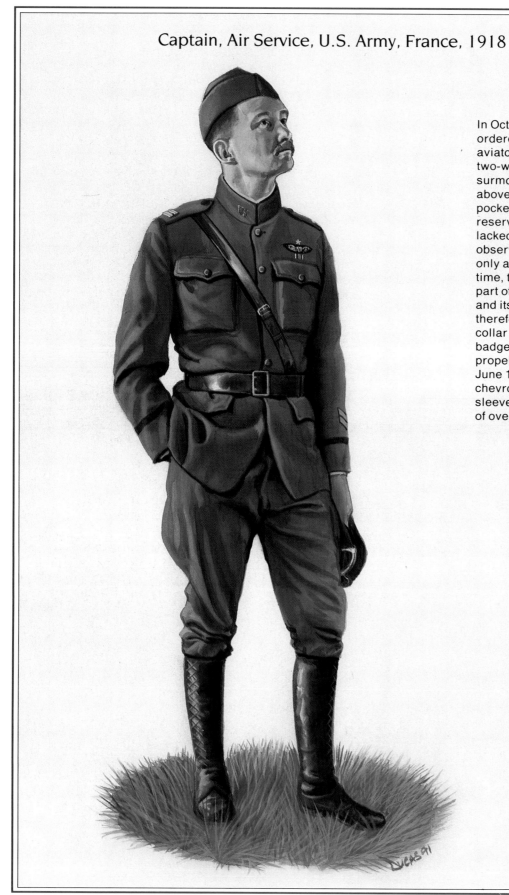

In October 1917, it was ordered that military aviators were to wear a two-winged shield surmounted by a star above the left breast pocket. Junior and reserve military aviators lacked the star, and the observer's shield had only a single wing. At the time, the Air Service was part of the Signal Corps, and its personnel therefore wore the corps' collar insignia. A collar badge of wings and a propeller was adopted in June 1918. The two chevrons on the lower left sleeve indicate one year of overseas service.

dorff to urge peace on Kaiser Wilhelm II, the mood of the German commanders later became less pessimistic.

The Battle Goes On

On the ground in the Meuse-Argonne offensive, every day the American divisions pushed forward a few hundred yards against strengthening German resistance, as additional divisions (27 by the end of the offensive) were thrown into the defense. The main limitation on American options was the slow pace of the 77th and 28th Divisions through the Foret d'Argonne. Efforts to clear the forest by probes inward from the edges failed, and small units found themselves pushing forward virtually from tree to tree. The French tried to help from the west, but they were as hampered by the

atrocious conditions and the German defense as I Corps' right-hand formation, the 35th Division, was. This unit, operating on the eastern side of the Foret d'Argonne, found after good initial progress through Varennes and Cheppy that it was suffering enfilading fire from German forces still deeply embedded in the Foret d'Argonne. As this part of the American offensive pushed slowly toward Baulny and Apremont, the 35th Division was replaced by the 1st Division.

The three factors that had the greatest effect on operations were the forest's steep and practically unclimbable ravines, the combination of constant rain with occasional fog, and the mass of wire entanglements matted into the heavy undergrowth. The first meant that units could not follow the lines of advance that had been planned for them, even when they were able to fix their own positions

American soldiers move off toward the front in French railroad cars.

This picture of the ruins of Cambrai on October 19, 1918 illustrates the devastating effect of war upon the French towns.

exactly. The second combined with the terrain to make communication with either rear headquarters or flanking units next to impossible, and the third prevented any practical coordinated movement.

The effect of these factors was fully understood by October 2. On that day,

Pershing ordered his units not even to try to keep in touch with each other. Instead they should push straight ahead, holding any positions they captured. The result, Pershing hoped, would be a network of American positions from which the remaining German strongpoints could be mopped up, once the U.S. troops had

Pack animals worked as well as wheeled vehicles as transportation in difficult and shell-torn terrain during World War I. This American donkey train is shown moving up to the Foret d'Argonne.

American troops on the move in the St. Mihiel area during October 1918.

begun to emerge from the forest. The 1st Army's commander also hoped that the tactic would distract the Germans in the forest enough that the artillery and machinegun attacks on the left flank of V Corps would fade away.

A good example of the results of Pershing's order is the episode of "the lost battalion." An element of the 77th Division, this battalion of 550 men was commanded by Major Charles W. Whittlesey, a quiet-spoken man who had been a lawyer before joining the army. Between September 28 and October 1, the battalion had already been nearly isolated from the rest of the division, but in accordance with Pershing's new instructions, it moved deeper into the forest on the following day and headed for the Charlevaux valley. The battalion's nine companies encountered little resistance in reaching their objective and immediately dug in as best they could.

Whittlesey appreciated that the flanking battalions had probably met stiffer resistance and were therefore farther back, when German voices were heard behind the battalion, it became clear that the American soldiers had been cut off. The men had little ammunition, few rations, and no way of communicating with the rest of their regiment, and the Americans soon discovered that the Germans had cut their line of withdrawal with a screen of barbed wire and machine guns.

Further evidence that the Germans knew of the battalion's presence arrived shortly in the form of an artillery and mortar bombardment. The soldiers lacked the equipment to dig artillery-proof trenches in the hard ground, and casualties began to mount. The Germans, it was later discovered, thought at first that they had trapped a company, which they hoped to force into surrender with artillery and mortar fire alone. They still

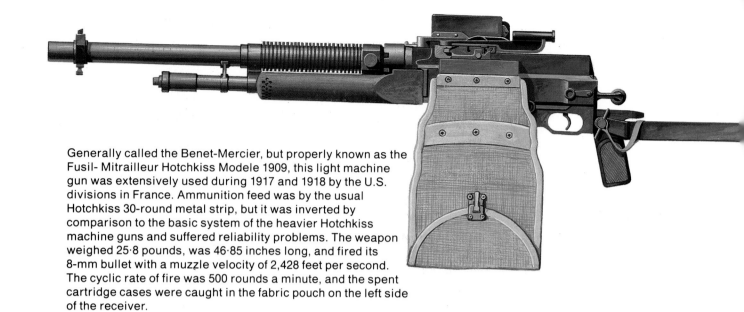

Generally called the Benet-Mercier, but properly known as the Fusil- Mitrailleur Hotchkiss Modele 1909, this light machine gun was extensively used during 1917 and 1918 by the U.S. divisions in France. Ammunition feed was by the usual Hotchkiss 30-round metal strip, but it was inverted by comparison to the basic system of the heavier Hotchkiss machine guns and suffered reliability problems. The weapon weighed 25·8 pounds, was 46·85 inches long, and fired its 8-mm bullet with a muzzle velocity of 2,428 feet per second. The cyclic rate of fire was 500 rounds a minute, and the spent cartridge cases were caught in the fabric pouch on the left side of the receiver.

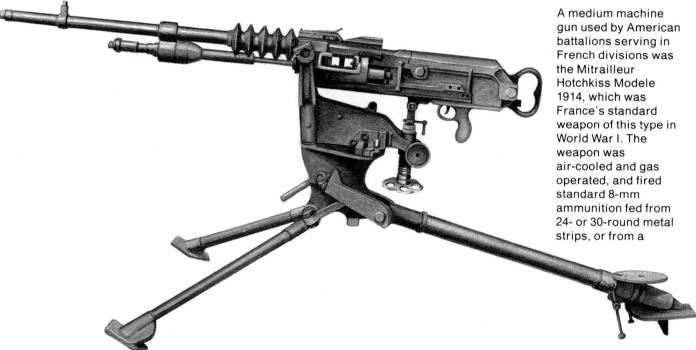

A medium machine gun used by American battalions serving in French divisions was the Mitrailleur Hotchkiss Modele 1914, which was France's standard weapon of this type in World War I. The weapon was air-cooled and gas operated, and fired standard 8-mm ammunition fed from 24- or 30-round metal strips, or from a 249-round "strip belt" made from three-round "striplets." The gun weighed 52 pounds and was 50 inches long. The bullet was fired with a muzzle velocity of 2,379 feet per second, and the rate of fire was between 400 and 600 rounds a minute.

considered this tactic adequate even after they discovered that their target was a battalion. Whittlesey had already refused to consider retreat as he had been ordered to take and hold ground, and he now refused the Germans' demands for surrender. The approximate position of the battalion was known to its parent division, but the only way that supplies could be delivered was by parachute, but all such loads fell outside the battalion's perimeter. Nine men made unauthorized efforts to bring in the supplies, but all were killed or captured – one was blindfolded and returned to the battalion with a surrender demand.

By this time, the battalion was in a desperate condition, with the wounded dying in increasing numbers for lack of medical care, the rest of the battalion

suffering from exposure, and everyone forced to eat grass and leaves. Whittlesey understood that divisional headquarters knew his approximate position, but probably not his exact location and perhaps not the condition of his command. He had four homing pigeons: three were sent out with messages, but were shot down by the Germans. The battalion then came in for still more trouble as American guns started to shell its area, and the last pigeon was launched with a desperate message. As this last bird, named Cher Ami (Dear Friend), set off to the rear, the Germans opened fire, breaking one leg and the breastbone, and also damaging a wing. The bird spiraled down, but then to the amazement of the watching American soldiers, regained control just above the trees and set off once more: soon, the

American barrage was lifted. Cher Ami was treated and sent to the United States, but died a year later.

The Germans realized that artillery and mortar fire alone were not enough to defeat the battalion and started to throw in infantry assaults. Repulsing these efforts exhausted the battalion's ammunition almost completely. Several runners sent out previously to contact division had already been killed or captured, but a final effort by PFC Abraham Krotoshinsky succeeded, and five days after the battalion had been trapped, the 194 survivors were reached by a relief force that had driven through the German besiegers.

By October 3, the American divisions had taken less than half of the Foret d'Argonne, but farther east they had pushed beyond the two defense lines of

Popularly known to the Germans as Dicke Bertha (generally translated as "Big Bertha" but more properly as "Fat Bertha"), this 420-mm howitzer was mobile, but was intended mainly for static use. The whole equipment weighed 75 tons and fired its truly devastating 2,052-pound projectile to a maximum range of 15,530 yards.

U.S. artillery observers spot the fall of their battery's shells. The men are making use of the ruins of a fortified artillery observation position abandoned by the retreating Germans.

the *Michel Stellung*. The farthest advance took place on the extreme right wing, where the 33rd Division advanced down the left bank of the Meuse River about six miles from where it had started. By now, the front-line divisions were exhausted and had lost the momentum of their advance, and Pershing sensibly called a temporary halt to the offensive along the line between Apremont and Brieulles. At this time, the American front-line formations were, from west to east, the 77th, 28th, and 1st Divisions of I Corps, the 91st, 32nd, and 3rd Divisions of V Corps, and the 4th and 33rd Divisions of III Corps.

The halt in the offensive was only temporary, but it allowed Pershing to replace the hardest-hit of the 1st Army's divisions with the veteran formations which had been resting behind the front. The pause also allowed the Germans to reinforce their front line, however, so not

even the introduction of more experienced divisions could materially alter the situation in which the American forces now found themselves. They were opposed by a steady defense and, sandwiched between the Meuse and the Foret d'Argonne, had no room to maneuver. Pershing and his men knew that they were now faced with the type of warfare that had long been the norm for the other Allied powers: set-piece attacks against a wily enemy fighting on ground of his own choice and well prepared with defensive features.

The offensive got under way again in its second phase, which started on October 4. During this second phase of the Meuse-Argonne operation, the 1st Army battered its way forward in series of frontal attacks that were given no scope for tactical flair by the difficulty of the terrain. The worst of the fighting was again in the Foret d'Argonne, where coordination of

An American 75-mm gun in action, October, 1918.

all but the smallest bodies of men was still impossible.

On the American right, the overall situation was eased by a widening of the offensive onto the eastern bank of the Meuse River. Pershing had now realized that an advance here would deprive the Germans of the observation and artillery positions for their flanking fire into III Corps and, to a lesser extent, V Corps. The control of this portion of a widened offensive demanded additional command capability, and on October 12, Pershing created a 2nd Army to oversee operations south of Haudiomont, which lies southeast of Verdun. The army's task was to extend the offensive to the northeast, toward the line of the Moselle River. The commander of this new army was Bullard of III Corps, and his two subordinate formations were IV and VI Corps, as well as a French corps that included the 33rd division in its strength. IV Corps controlled the 28th and 7th Divisions, and though it had been commanded by Dickman up to this time, under the new appointments, its commander became Major General Muir. VI Corps was created only on October 23 under the command of Major General Ballou, who was succeeded on November 10 by Major General Menoher; the corps' main American asset was the 92nd Division.

On October 12, Liggett left I Corps to become 1st Army commander, and Pershing again became commander-in-chief of the American Expeditionary Force, which now became a U.S. Army group. From this time, command of I, III, and V Corps passed respectively to Major Generals Dickman, Summerall, and Hines.

Advances were made on a slow but continuous basis. The progress along the eastern bank of the Meuse River by XVII Corps, an attached Franco-American formation under French command on

Lacking tanks of indigenous design and manufacture, the Americans laid plans for an extremely ambitious program of design and manufacture in collaboration mainly with the British. The planners realized that this program would not yield results until 1919, so the first U.S. tank units were equipped with the best light tank of the period, the FT 1917, produced by the French company Renault. The FT 1917 has a good claim to being the first modern tank, for it carried a turret capable of traverse through 360° and had most of its internal components built directly into the hull to remove the need for a chassis. This simplified the vehicle, reduced its weight and, by eliminating the butted and strapped joints of contemporary tanks of the day, reduced its chances of suffering from ''splash.'' This happened when lead from bullets hit the tank, half-melted, and splashed through imperfect joints to reach the inside of the vehicle, causing many casualties. The FT 1917 weighed 6·5 tons, was 16½ feet long, and carried a crew of two (commander/gunner and driver). The 39-horsepower Renault engine provided a maximum speed of 5 miles an hour, and its range was 37 miles. Armament was a 37-mm gun with 240 rounds of ammunition or an 8-mm machine gun with 4,800 rounds. In addition to French vehicles, U.S. forces also used an American-built version that differed only slightly from the French original, but had a 42-horsepower Budo engine. Orders were placed for 4,400 of these vehicles, but only about 1,000 were built with the designation 6 Ton M1917 Tank, used mainly in the early 1920s.

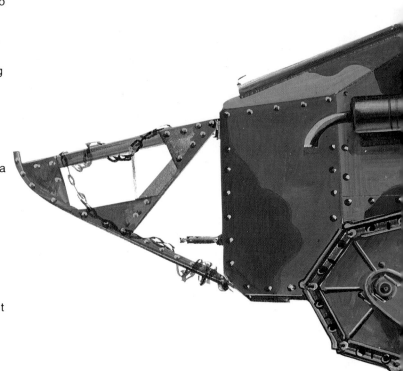

the right wing of the 1st Army, finally deprived the Germans of their flanking artillery positions. The three American formations in this corps were the 26th, 79th, and 81st Divisions.

On the left flank of the offensive, the 2nd Division, attached to the French 4th Army, took the high ground of Blanc Mont on October 5 in a move that finally persuaded the Germans in front of the 4th Army to fall back toward the Aisne River. On October 10, I Corps finally cleared the Foret d'Argonne, after very heavy fighting right up to the last hours.

Another celebrated episode of the fighting in the Foret d'Argonne took place near Chatel-Chehery on October 8. A patrol of Company G, 328th Infantry Regiment, 82nd Division, surprised and captured a party of about 75 Germans. The American patrol was shepherding its prisoners back toward the rear when it too was surprised, this time by German machine gunners. The initial German bursts killed or wounded nine of the 17 Americans, and a German lieutenant then prepared his men to charge the surviving members of the American patrol. As the Germans advanced, a Tennessee marksman, PFC Alvin C. York, steadily shot 15 of them, and then, at the head of the surviving seven men, charged the German position. The rest of the Germans surrendered after a sharp firefight. It was later established that York's skill and heroism had resulted in the capture of several machine guns as well as 132 Germans (four officers and 128 other ranks). York was awarded an exceptionally well merited Medal of Honor. But there was no rest for the 1st Army as a whole. During the rest of the month, its divisions fought their way forward toward the Germans' main defense lines through

the steep hills and valleys separating the Foret d'Argonne from the Meuse. Only on the last day of the month did the 1st Army finally break through the last part of the *Freya und Brunhilde Stellungen* to reach a west/east line between Grand Pre and Bantheville, where the line swerved south to meet the Meuse River at Sivry-sur-Mieuse.

At this time, the deployment of American corps was, from west to east, I Corps with the 78th, 77th, and 80th Divisions, V Corps with the 2nd and 89th Divisions, and III Corps with the 90th, 5th, and 33rd Divisions.

Georges Clemenceau, the French prime minister, had become increasingly unhappy with what he saw as slow American progress and tried to persuade the administration that Pershing should be replaced by a more determined and aggressive commander. But Clemenceau did not have the support even of Foch, who saw clearly what the American forces had achieved in terms of attracting German attention and reserves, if not in gaining ground. Even though its advance was not as fast or far as Allied command had hoped, the 1st Army had sucked in large numbers of German reserve formations (27 divisions in all) as Ludendorff attempted to safeguard Mezieres. Foch knew full well that this fighting had eased the task of the Allied forces pressing forward elsewhere along the Western Front. Pershing's position was safe, and the American commander in Europe set about coordinating the final phase of the Meuse-Argonne offensive with Liggett's 1st Army and Bullard's 2nd Army.

The major effort was to be made by a rejuvenated 1st Army along a 12-mile front. From left to right, it involved the three first-line divisions of Dickman's I Corps, the two first-line divisions of Summerall's V Corps, and the three first-line divisions of Hines's III Corps. On the eastern side of the Meuse River, General de Corps d'Armee Claudel's XVII Corps deployed its one French and two American divisions for a further expansion of the Allied drive with an advance that would wheel from north to northeast in an effort to reach the road linking Damvillers and Jametz.

To the southeast, the 2nd Army prepared its one French and two American corps for a limited advance that would pin the German defense in front of them and thereby prevent movement of major reinforcements to the Meuse-Argonne region.

On October 4, the new German chancellor had cabled Washington requesting an armistice. Wilson did not inform the Allied governments of the German move, but instead asked the Germans for clarification of their request. The chancellor replied on October 12, saying that Germany agreed to Wilson's "Fourteen Points." By this time, word of the German peace overture had reached the Allied governments, and the British and French in particular were in no way prepared to accept Wilson's unilateral negotiation with Germany. Ludendorff had meanwhile recovered from the deep gloom that had afflicted him since September 28 and, seeing that the Allies were not routing the German armies in the way he had feared, he suggested to the Kaiser that the time was ripe to ask for terms that would allow Germany to pull her armies back behind the German frontier. There, the armies could regain their strength, and Germany would thus be in a position to refuse any Allied demands that she thought excessive.

American wounded watch German soldiers march into captivity during October 1918.

Left: A U.S. tank unit advances near Boureilles during the Meuse-Argonne offensive.

Below: An American 14-inch railway gun in action, September, 1918.

American soldiers search a German before sending him back to captivity in a prisoner-of-war camp.

Events were taking the initiative from the Germans once more, however. Continued Allied advances revealed the brutal savagery with which the Germans had destroyed the regions through which they were retreating, and Allied opinion again hardened against Germany. This tendency was reinforced by the continued U-boat campaign. On October 10, a passenger steamer was sunk off the coast of Ireland with the loss of 300 lives, and just a few days later, an Irish mail boat was hit with the loss of 520 passengers, most of them women and children. Messages were still being exchanged between Washington and Berlin, but stopped on October 23 when Wilson cabled that the United States and the Allies would not negotiate an armistice with the German military dictatorship. As the American

message put it, if the United States had to treat "with the military masters and the monarchial autocrats of Germany now, or if it is likely to have to deal with them later in regard to the international obligations of the German Empire, it must demand, not peace negotiations but surrender."

Ludendorff demanded that Germany reject the American and Allied terms, but the Kaiser and his government were completely disillusioned by military reverses, the threat of mutiny in the navy, rioting in the streets of Germany's starving cities, and the growing threat of Bolshevik revolution within the country. On October 27, Ludendorff learned that he was about to be dismissed. He resigned and fled in disguise to Sweden. The Kaiser refused to dismiss von Hindenburg, who remained as commander-in-chief, and appointed

Above: Defeating the menace of the U-boats was a long and particularly arduous task that had lasted throughout World War I. Allied and American sailors watched with great relief as *U-108* and *U-113* lay in Brest harbor after surrendering in November 1918.

Left: In addition to their main gun armament, most U.S. destroyers carried 6-pounder light guns. They had a high rate of fire, and though they fired only a small and comparatively short-range projectile, they proved effective at punching holes in U-boats.

Above: One of the last U.S. destroyers built before the advent of the definitive flush-decked classes, the U.S.S. *Wadsworth*, the fourth unit of the 12-strong "Tucker" class, was launched on March 29, 1915. The 1,060-ton ship was active in anti-submarine operations; her primary armament included four 4-inch guns and eight 21-inch torpedo tubes.

Right: A U.S. convoy in a dazzle camouflage scheme, designed not to improve each ship's chances of avoiding detection, but to make it more difficult for the U-boat commander to assess the ship's course, speed, and size.

Operations in British waters could be very cold, especially during winter, and U.S. sailors were issued with lambswool coats such as the one shown here.

General Wilhelm Groener as the new quartermaster-general. On October 29, the mutiny of the High Seas Fleet in Germany's northern ports led to disorder, mutiny, and revolution in Germany.

The Meuse-Argonne offensive started again on November 1, the third phase of the campaign. The infantry advanced after a short but very sharp artillery barrage. In the center of the 1st Army's front, V Corps made the best progress. During the first day, they covered about six miles, extending the American line in a northward bulge that reached the heights overlooking the German fourth defensive line near Barricourt.

The scale and determination of this advance persuaded the Germans that it was senseless to attempt to hold their positions southwest of the Meuse River. Over the next few days, the Germans pulled back toward the river under continued American pressure. By November 3, all three American corps had pushed forward another three or more miles, and the 2nd Division of V corps had made a startling advance well forward of its flanking divisions to reach a point just south of Beaumont. III Corps forced a crossing of the Meuse south of Stenay on November 5, and soon afterward units of V Corps also pressed across this river barrier farther to the north, in the area southeast of Mouzon. On the Americans' extreme left, the 42nd Division of I Corps reached the heights above the Meuse

WHAT THE NAVY IS DOING

DEPTH BOMBS DEAL DEATH TO U-BOATS

For this Hun the war is over, blown to bits by a depth bomb planted at the right time. It is the merry little depth bomb—in destroyer lingo, "the ash can" which upends the Kaiser's subs and puts them to sleep on the ocean bed. Containing a heavy charge of explosive, the bomb is dropped and explodes at a set depth. In this case the bomb must have been dropped before the U-boat dove over it, the explosion lifting the sub's bow upwards and tearing it to pieces.

A poster for the navy reserve and coast guards showing the effects of a ''trash can'' depth charge.

River opposite Sedan on November 8.

The arrival of the American forces along the river allowed their artillery to start to cut the main railroad line between Mezieres and Montmedy, a vital artery of supply for the entire German front line. The 1st Division was preparing for a final dash to Sedan when high-level Allied orders revealed that the honor of retaking the city must fall to a French formation. Plans were quickly prepared on November 10 to shift the 1st Army's axis of advance farther east in the direction of Longwy near the Belgian frontier,

German prisoners move off toward the rear past a pair of American truck-mounted antiaircraft guns.

Named "Calamity Jane," this gun fired the last Allied shot of World War I.

and the 2nd Army's axis toward Briey.

On November 7, a German civil delegation had started armistice talks with the Allied high command at Compiegne. Germany's new socialist government had declared Germany a republic on November 10, and the following day, the Armistice brought hostilities to an end at 11.00 a.m.

At this time, the Americans were along or across the Meuse River between Sedan and Stenay, and well past it between Stenay and a point east of Vacherauville. From northwest to southeast, the front-line formations of the 1st Army were the 42nd and 77th Divisions of I Corps, the 1st, 2nd, and 89th Divisions of V Corps, the 90th, 5th, and 32nd Divisions of III Corps. Another seven American divisions of the 2nd Army's one French and two American corps were also in the front line, and there were other American divisions in the line with British and French armies.

So the greatest American battle of World War I ended. In all, some 1,250,000 men had been involved. About 120,000 men had become casualties (killed, wounded, or otherwise injured), a large number by any standard. The result was impressive, however; this was the battle that worried German commanders most in the closing days of the war. Unlike

other sectors of the front, the Germans could not trade space for time in the Meuse-Argonne area because of the threat posed by the American forces to the vital lateral rail line that served the whole German effort and ran so close behind their front line.

The number of men who served in the American forces between April 6, 1917, and November 11, 1918, was 4,734,991 (4,057,101 in the army and the rest in the navy and marines). This strength suffered 53,402 battle deaths (50,510 in the army, 431 in the navy, and 2,461 in the marines), 63,114 other deaths (55,868 in the army, 6,856 in the navy, and 390 in the marines), and 204,002 wounded (193,663 in the army, 819 in the navy, and 9,520 in the marines).

As these casualty figures suggest, the part played by the U.S. Navy in World War I was considerably smaller than that played by the army. Nevertheless, it was very important. Five vessels of the American battleship squadron served with the Grand Fleet, and another three American battleships operated in Irish waters against the threat of German surface raiders. Perhaps more significantly, 79 American destroyers were involved in the all-important convoy role in the Atlantic, and 135 smaller sub-

On Armistice Day, President Wilson read to Congress the terms of the armistice agreement imposed upon the Germans with effect from the 11th hour of the 11th day of the 11th month of 1918.

marine chasers operated in European waters. Another major success for the navy was the laying of 56,000 of the 70,000 mines that formed the North Sea mine field between Scotland and Norway. This belt was 75 percent complete at the end of the war and effectively bottled German ships into the North Sea. The first half of 1919 was spent sweeping this field clear of the mines.

Under the terms of the Armistice agreement, Germany immediately handed over vast quantities of materiel (including 5,000 guns and 25,000 machine guns), surrendered all submarines, interned all other warships under the direction of the Allies (from November 21), and started the evacuation of all occupied territory, including Alsace-Lorraine (from November 17). Another provision of the agreement was the establishment of corridors across western Germany leading to bridgeheads across the Rhine River. These zones each had a radius of 18 miles on

the eastern side of the waterway and were occupied on December 9 after American and Allied forces had entered the Rhineland on December 1. The Belgians had the northern corridor, the British and French held corridors and associated bridgeheads centered on Koln and Mainz, and the Americans used their newly created 3rd Army to occupy the central corridor and bridgehead at Koblenz. This task demanded the initial deployment of nine divisions, but after the conclusion of the Treaty of Versailles in May 1919, the American presence was rapidly scaled down. The Senate refused to ratify the Treaty of Versailles; a joint Congressional declaration on May 20, 1919, finally formally ended the state of war between the United States on the one side and Germany and Austria-Hungary on the other. Separate peace treaties with Germany, Austria, and Hungary were concluded on October 18, 1920.

Even so, by the beginning of 1920,

French peasants greet the U.S. soldiers who liberated their village of Brielles sur Bar. The soldier on the left is carrying a French weapon used in some quantity by the U.S. divisions in France. Generally known as the Chauchat and universally disliked for its unreliability and very poor manufacture, this light machine gun was properly known as the Fusil Mitrailleur Modele 1915 Chauchat Sutter Ribeyrolle-Gladiator. The magazine was a 20-round box carried under the weapon and was so curved that it was virtually semi-circular.

there were only 15,000 American soldiers in Germany. The strength of the American forces in Germany was steadily reduced, and on January 23, 1923, the last 1,000 American soldiers in Germany turned their sector over to the French. The following day, these soldiers started on their way home. One American regiment had been sent to Italy before the collapse of Austria-Hungary, and for a period of four months, it was involved in the occupation of Austria.

American forces were also involved in two areas of Russia. In the first three years of the war, the Allies had poured vast quantities of supplies into Russia to help equip the Tsarist armies that were very large, but very poorly equipped. Most of these supplies reached Russia though the northern ports of Murmansk and Archangel, and the eastern port of Vladivostok, in an effort that peaked in 1916 and the first part of 1917. The indifferent nature of the Russian

transportation system meant that a large part of this physical aid was still in supply dumps near these ports at the time of the Russian revolution at the end of 1917. The size of these dumps was huge: at Vladivostok, there were 750,000 tons of goods valued at more than $750,000,000.

The Bolshevik revolution of November 1917 overthrew the moderate Kerensky government that had come to power after the revolution of March 1917. Under the leadership of Vladimir Ilyich Ulyanov, known as Lenin, the new government started the peace process with the Central Powers. The Allies were deeply concerned that the Germans might be able to seize, or force the Bolsheviks to hand over, the stockpiles of American and Allied supplies. The situation was complicated by the contemptuous attitude of the Bolsheviks to the Americans and Allies, and by the presence in western Siberia of the Czech Legion. This 100,000-man force, made up of

French women decorate the graves of American dead in Brest during 1918.

Bohemian deserters and prisoners from the Austro-Hungarian army who had joined the Tsarist army, had since June 1918 been trying to return home by fighting their way along the Trans-Siberian Railroad which ran to Vladivostok.

The first of the powers to intervene in Russia was Japan, which acted unilaterally and not as an agent of the United States or the Allied nations. On April 5, 1918, a small landing was made at Vladivostok, but it soon pulled out again. However, on August 3, the Japanese started to land their 12th Division at Vladivostok as part of a plan that saw the delivery of 70,000 or more Japanese soldiers by November. Under the command of General Otami, this steadily reinforced Japanese army soon occupied the Russian Maritime Provinces, stirring considerable alarm in Washington, Paris, and London, where it was assumed that this was the first step in a Japanese annexation of Russia's

eastern possessions. In the short term, however, the Japanese presence in Siberia safeguarded the stockpiles of American and Allied supplies in Vladivostok.

The dumps in Murmansk and Archangel were considerably nearer to the Germans. Allied unhappiness at the close proximity of the Germans to these stockpiles at the time of the armistice of Brest-Litovsk in December 1917 was already great, but in February 1918, the Germans responded to Soviet prevarication in the following treaty negotiations by plunging deeper into Russia. Thus the Allies thought it would be prudent to secure the stockpiles of their equipment as soon as possible.

On June 23, 1918, a mainly British and French expeditionary force, which included about 5,000 Americans of a three-battalion reinforced infantry regiment, began to land at Murmansk. Under British command, this force occupied the area and then moved to seize the Archan-

U.S. soldiers (one of them on guard) keep watch on the Rhine River on December 12, 1918, after the arrival of American forces in the German city of Koblenz.

gel region on August 1-2. The Soviets moved quite swiftly to contain this threat, which they sensibly felt might lead to an Allied effort to drive south and link up with the Czech Legion. The allied force was checked on the line of the Vologda River, and for more than a year, there was a small, undeclared but hard-fought war in this area. The heart of the United States had never been in this intervention, and in August 1919, the American force was pulled out, a few weeks before the British and French also abandoned Archangel and Murmansk.

There was greater American interest in an intervention in Siberia, overtly for the humanitarian reason of aiding the Czech Legion, and less obviously to check Japan's ambitions. In August 1918, an American force of 10,000 men, the 27th and 31st Infantry Regiments under the command of Major General William S. Graves, landed in Vladivostok. Graves had specific orders not to interfere in Russian domestic politics, but to concentrate on helping the Czech Legion to reach Vladivostok. Graves faced great difficulties, for he was soon at logger-heads not only with the Japanese, but also with the British and French intervention forces, the Red forces of the Bolsheviks, and the counterrevolutionary White forces led by Admiral Kolchak.

Tension between the Japanese and Americans frequently threatened to lead to conflict, but was always averted by Graves's diplomacy. The other interventionist forces expected the Americans to cooperate with support for the Whites, but Graves steadfastly refused to consider any such thing. The American force operated along the Trans-Siberian Railroad as far west as Lake Baikal, often becoming involved in actions with Russian forces, both White and Red, in the process. The effort of Kolchak's White forces finally collapsed, and the Americans held the railroad

Men of the 64th Infantry Regiment salute the news of the Armistice.

until the Czech Legion had reached Vladivostok and embarked. Only then, in April 1920, did the Americans pull out of Siberia and return home.

While these legacies of World War I were being played out by small forces, the United States was trying to demobilize its vast wartime force and decide on the future nature of its armed forces. The end of World War I in November 1918 had taken the United States and the Allies by surprise, for all the senior military leaders thought that it would take sustained offensives during 1919 for the allied forces to drive into Germany and so compel the Germans to surrender. In the United States, planning for demobilization began only one month before the Armistice, which made most officers and men in the forces eligible for discharge. With by far the largest number of men under arms, the War Department faced a greater problem than the Navy Department. It was now faced with the practical difficulties of mustering these men out as quickly and fairly as possible without completely disrupting the national economy, and at the same time maintaining a smaller yet effective army for such postwar duties as the occupation of the American sector in Germany.

The War Department decided that the best answer was the time-honored method of demobilization by unit. Units in the United States were moved to 30 demob centers dotted across the country, so that men could be processed and discharged near their homes. Overseas units were brought back to the United States as fast as transportation could be arranged, processed in debarkation centers operated by the Transportation Service, and then moved to demobilization centers for final discharge. It is worth noting, however, that the unit demobilization system was complemented by individual and occupational group demobilizations, the latter made up mainly of railroad workers and anthracite coal miners.

In the first full month of demobilization, the army discharged 650,000 officers and men. Within nine months, the total had grown to 3,250,000 officers and men without any significant disruption of the national economy. Over the same period, war industry was demobilized. Surplus materiel was put up for disposal, with the exception of a large weapon reserve which the army stockpiled for use in peace or sudden war emergency. Despite its lack of advance planning on a comprehensive scale, the War Department completed the demobilization process with commendable skill.

At the beginning of the demob process, the army was worried because it lacked the authority to enlist new men to replace those who were being demobilized. Soon after the end of World War I, the War Department had recommended a regular army strength of about 600,000, as well as a three-month universal training system that would allow quick and effective expansion in times of emergency. The concept was immediately rejected by public and political opinion. There was a widespread belief that the defeat of the Central Powers and the exhaustion of all Europe in terms of manpower, industry, economy, and spirit heralded a period of prolonged peace. This applied particularly to land warfare, though more far-sighted Americans saw the possibility of naval conflict with Japan

for dominance of the Pacific Ocean.

A law of February 28, 1919, then gave the army the power to enlist men for one or three years. By the end of 1919, the army was again a force of regular volunteers with a strength of about 224,000 (19,000 officers and 205,000 enlisted men).

One of Wilson's "Fourteen Points" had paved the way for a prototype United Nations organization. This League of Nations was one of the most important results of the Treaty of Versailles. However, the Senate refused to ratify the treaty, and the United States thereby signaled its intention to avoid any active or cooperative involvement

Overjoyed U.S. soldiers arrive in Hoboken, New Jersey, on their way to demobilization.

President Wilson salutes the French crowd after his arrival in Paris for the beginning of the negotiations that led to the Treaty of Versailles.

in an international organization dedicated to the creation and maintenance of global security. This isolationist attitude was largely responsible for the limitation of the army to a size large enough only for the defense of the United States together with its limited overseas territories and possessions.

Considerable thought was given to the nature and scale of American defense needs, which resulted in the National Defense Act of June 4, 1920. This legislation was in essence a major amendment of the 1916 National Defense Act and is the most important piece of legislation affecting the American military establishment between the War of 1812 and the Korean War.

The main effect of the 1920 National Defense Act was to eliminate the concept of an expandable regular army. Instead, the act created an Army of the United States as an organization with three components, namely a professional Regular Army, a civilian National Guard, and civilian Organized Reserves (Officers' and Enlisted Reserve Corps). Within this basic structure, each component would be organized in peacetime so that in war it would contribute its proper proportion of the overall strength. The 1920 National Defense Act finally killed the notion of an

expandable regular army. Instead, it openly recognized what had long been the case: the small regular army was too small to be easily expanded to meet the needs of a major war, so in major wars, it had to be complemented by a larger army of civilian volunteers.

The training of this civilian component therefore became a major peacetime function of the army for the first time, and the army was given a maximum officer strength of 17,726, more than three times the army's real strength in officers before World War I. The act also laid down that at least half of the new officers were to be selected from non-regulars who had seen service during the war. At the same time, it established that, with the exception of doctors and chaplains, all promotions were to be made from a single list as a means of equalizing promotion opportunities. The enlisted strength of the army was limited to 280,000 men, though actual strength in enlisted men as well as officers would depend on the annual appropriation voted by Congress.

The 1920 National Defense Act authorized the army to keep all its established branches, and to add three new ones: the Finance Department, the Air Service, and the Chemical Warfare

A young soldier, Howad Munder of the 28th Infantry Division, participated in the Second Battle of the Maine. His letter describes how green American troops became veterans.

Dear Mother and Dad:
Received last night your letter of the 24th of June it certainly came at a time when I needed it the most. The news it contained made me very happy and contented to think my letters are appreciated so much. It was the only thing I needed to brace me up and believe me I needed bracing very badly. Since last Sunday night I have been under a continuous rain of shells from the German batteries on the opposite side of the hill. Also to make things worse a continuous machine gun and gas shell firing followed by heavy rains. On the line here, we have rain every hour, due to the artillery. This is also made worse by dozens of German planes dropping bombs on us only inches away. This warfare is quite exciting. At first I was scared nearly stiff and jumped as though shot when shells went off near me. Now I am getting somewhat used to them and when I hear a wiz, I just duck flat on my stomach and lay a few seconds after the shell has struck. I have had shells strike only 20 feet away, not touching anybody in our party. Also had an airbomb drop within 25 feet; except for showering us with dirt it did no further harm. Day before yesterday a shell hit only 18 feet away from me, knocking me flat on my back and making me lose a whole plate of honest to goodness American beans.

I certainly think God is protecting me, because many have left us for good, including our Y.M.C.A. man Mr. Murry, who was hit by an exploding shell as he came from the Hospital where he was helping our wounded boys.

Last night we had a fearful wind, rain and electric storm. It was something awful. Today we are drying out and trying to get some sleep before tonight's activities. Yesterday for the first time I saw huge tanks in action. I also saw several aeroplane battles in which one plane crashed to the ground, coming down in circles and the other two came in a huge cloud of flames and smoke. Yesterday they brought five hundred German prisoners past us. Taking them to the rear. A lot of the boys got souvenirs from them, as they all were made to turn out their pockets.

July 20, 1918
Dear Mother and Dad;
Just a few lines to let you know I am well and happy with not a single cut on me. Our regiment just returned from the trenches, after holding one of the most dangerous positions along the entire front. The regiment has made a name for itself and will go down in history as the regiment of iron which held the Germans from breaking through the last defense. We held the Germans under terrific shell fire for four days till the French and our own men and artillery could reinforce us.

They talk about hell on earth. Nothing can be more hell than artillery fire for several hours, in fact days, without let up. I only thank God for His gracious care and protection. Many comrades cease to live among us.

Things on the front are much more encouraging. The Germans are held all along a 60 mile front and in some places beat back severely.

I am going to close now and don't worry, for I am not sick, wounded or shell shocked, but am well, happy and thankful.
    Ever lovingly,
        Your devoted son,
            Howard.

On June 14, 1919, General Pershing entertained senior commanders at lunch at his headquarters, the Chateau Val des Ecolters at Chaumont in the Departement de Haute-Marne. From left to right, the officers in the front row are Brigadier General McCoy, Lieutenant General Hunter Liggett, Marshal Petain, General Pershing, Major General J.W. McAndrew, and Brigadier General L.R. Hollbrock.

Service. The addition of the two new services recognized the importance demonstrated by these two new combat techniques in World War I. At the same time, the Tank Corps was incorporated into the Infantry, a move that seemed sensible in the light of tank use in World War I, but which hindsight showed to be less than far-sighted. In 1926, the Air Service became a combat arm in its own right as the Air Corps.

The 1920 National Defense Act instructed the War Department to undertake planning for mobilization and other war preparations, allocating the military parts of this task to the Chief of Staff and the General Staff, while planning and supervision of industrial procurement became the responsibility of the Assistant Secretary of War.

World War I had considerably enhanced the position and power of the General Staff. When Pershing became Chief of Staff in 1921, he reorganized the General Staff on the expanded basis of his A.E.F. staff in France with divisions responsible for personnel (G-1), intelligence (G-2), training and operations (G-3), supply (G-4), and war plans (G-5). The last was a new departure, and its tasks were strategic planning and planning against the eventuality of war. The War Plans Division originated a celebrated series of color-coded plans for war with particular countries and provided the basis for General Headquarters, which would provide operational direction in time of war.

Army forces inside the United States were allocated to nine corps headquarters, covering areas of roughly equal population. Forces in Panama, Hawaii, and the Philippines were allocated to departments with authority similar to the corps. The operational lessons of World War I were reflected in the fact that the division rather than the regiment now became the basic army unit, especially in terms of planning, and each corps had six divisions (one Regular Army, two National Guard, and three Reserve). A separate Cavalry Division was set up to patrol the Mexican border, and the mobile forces in Hawaii and the Philippines became the Hawaiian and Philippine Divisions.

New Yorkers give a typical welcome to U.S. soldiers home from France.

At the time that the 1920 National Defense Act became law, the army had a strength of about 200,000 men. In January 1921, Congress ordered that the strength be reduced to 175,000 men, and just five months later, to 150,000 men. In mid-1922, Congress limited the army to 12,000 officers and 125,enlisted men excluding the 7,000 of the Philippine Scouts, which stabilized the strength of the army up to 1936.

Glossary

Army group: The largest field formation, containing two or more armies.

Barrage: A curtain of sustained artillery fire used to seal off an enemy position.

Battalion: A basic subdivision of the regiment, generally less than 1,000 men and commanded by a lieutenant colonel.

Battle-cruiser: A close relative of the battleship. It carries the same weight of armament, but has lighter protection and is more powerful. It therefore has a considerably higher performance.

Battleship: A major ship of the period, with heavy armament and heavy protection.

Blockade: A naval campaign to cut off access by closing the enemy's ports and coast.

Brigade: A basic unit of the division, including two or more regiments and commanded by a brigadier general.

Bunker: An underground shelter, normally built of lumber, designed to provide protection from shell fire.

Camouflage: The use of concealment and/or disguise to minimize the possibility of detection and/or identification by the enemy.

Cantonments: Lodgings for troops on a base.

Conscript: A civilian inducted to the armed forces as a result of the draft system.

Corps: A primary component of the army, made up of two or more divisions and commanded in the U.S. Army by a major general, but in most other armies by a lieutenant general.

Creeping barrage: A barrage in which the fire of all participating units remains in the same relative position throughout. The barrage advances in steps of one line at a time, which allows infantry to follow closely behind it.

Cruiser: A long-range warship between the destroyer and the battleship in size. It has two basic forms: a light or unarmored cruiser with 6-inch guns for raiding merchant shipping and a heavy or armored type with guns of 8-inch or greater caliber for fleet operations.

Destroyer: A comparatively small warship developed from the torpedo boat. It has torpedoes and guns of about 5-inch caliber and is used for independent or fleet operations. The destroyer relies on speed and agility to avoid enemy fire, not on armor to withstand such fire.

Division: The smallest army formation, containing two or more brigades and commanded by a major general. It is the basic army organization used for independent operations and therefore contains support elements (artillery, engineers, etc.) in addition to its infantry.

Dreadnought battleship: Named after the first such ship, the British H.M.S. *Dreadnought* which was completed in 1906. The ultimate battleship, its substantial main battery featured guns of a single caliber generally mounted on the ship's centerline. The first American dreadnoughts were the U.S.S. *South Carolina* and U.S.S. *Michigan* of the "South Carolina" class. They had a main battery of eight 12-inch guns in four twin turrets and a secondary battery of twenty-two 3-inch guns.

Elastic defense: A defense based on hard and soft defense of sectors along the front, designed so that the enemy is tempted to advance through areas of soft defense and can then be taken in flank by the adjoining sectors of hard defense.

Fall-back party: A group given the task of holding a defensive position for a short time to allow a larger force to retreat without interference from the enemy.

Flank: The extreme right or left side of a body of troops in a military position.

Formation: Any large body of troops with a capability to operate independently from the rest of the army. It therefore possesses (in addition to its organic infantry units) a full range of artillery, engineer, and support services. The smallest formation is generally the division.

Interdiction: Isolating or sealing off an area, mainly to deny use of the area to the enemy as a line of approach to the battlefield.

Logistics: The science of planning and carrying out the movement of forces and their supplies.

Machine gun nest: A specially designed defensive position, with one or more machine guns protected by sandbags and barbed wire, and generally protected by entrenched infantry.

Materiel: The overall term for equipment, stores, supplies, and spares.

Mortar: A lightweight piece of ordnance designed to throw a comparatively light "bomb" (explosive-filled shell) over a short range with a high trajectory. Such "bombs" land almost vertically. In World War I, trench mortars were virtually the only front-line weapons able to deliver explosives into the enemy's trench lines.

Munitions: The overall term for weapons and ammunition.

Pre-dreadnought battleship: A battleship of the period before the dreadnought battleship came into service in 1906. Such ships were comparatively slow, but were moderately well armored and had a mixed main gun armament. The last two American pre-dreadnoughts were the U.S.S. *Mississippi* and U.S.S. *Idaho* of the "Mississippi" class. They had a main battery of four 12-inch guns in two twin turrets, eight 8-inch guns in four twin turrets, and eight 7-inch guns in single mountings, as well as a secondary battery of twelve 3-inch guns.

Regiment: A basic tactical unit subordinate to the brigade. It was made up of two or more battalions and generally commanded by a colonel.

Salient: An area that projects into enemy territory across the notional straight front line.

Strategy: The art of winning a campaign or war by major operations.

Tactics: The art of winning a battle by minor operations.

Unit: Any small body of troops which is not capable of operations independent of the rest of the army. It therefore does not possess a full range of artillery, engineer, and support services. The largest unit is the brigade.

Bibliography

American Armies and Battlefields in Europe.
(Government Printing Office, Washington, 1938).
A battlefield guide.

Cofman, Edward M. *The War to End All Wars.*
(University of Wisconsin Press, Madison, WI, 1986).

Esposito, Vincent J. (ed.). *The West Point Atlas of American Wars 1900-1953.*
(Frederick A. Praeger, New York, 1959).
A fine map book coordinated with easy-to-understand text.

Flammer, Philip M. *Vivid Air: The Lafayette Escadrille.*
(University of Georgia Press, Athens, GA, 1981).
U.S. aviators who volunteered to fly for France.

Friedel, Frank. *Over There: The Story of America's First Great Overseas Crusade.*
(Bramhall House, New York, 1964).

Gies, Joseph. *Crisis 1918.*
(W. W. Norton, New York, 1964).

Goldhurst, Richard. *Pipe Clay and Drill.*
(Thomas Y. Crowell Co., New York, 1977).
Biography of Pershing.

Graves, William S. *America's Siberian Adventure 1918-1920.*
Peter Smith, New York, 1941).
The Russian intervention.

Hoobler, Dorothy and Thomas. *The Trenches: Fighting on the Western Front in World War I.*
(G. P. Putnam's Sons, New York, 1978).
For younger readers.

Johnson, Thomas M. and Fletcher Pratt. *The Lost Battalion.*
(Bobbs-Merrill Co., New York, 1938).
An exciting account of this famous incident.

Marrin, Albert. *The Yanks Are Coming.*
(Atheneum, New York, 1986).

Matthews, William and Dixon Wecter. *Our Soldiers Speak 1775-1918.*
(Little Brown & Co., Boston, 1943).

Pershing, John J. *My Experiences in the World War.*
(Frederick A. Stokes Co., New York, 1931).
The personal account of the U.S. commander in Europe.

Pitt, Barrie. *1918: The Last Act.*
(Ballantine Books, New York, 1962).

Remarque, Erich Maria. *All Quiet on the Western Front.*
(Fawcett, Greenwich, CT, 1961).
The view from the other side, rightly considered a classic.

Rickenbacker, Capt. Eddie V. *Fighting the Flying Circus.*
(Doubleday & Co., Garden City, NY, 1965).
The story of one of America's most famous fighter pilots.

Simpson, Colin. *The Lusitania.*
(Little Brown, Boston, 1972).
The story of the U-boat attack and its effect on American policy.

Terraine, John. *The Great War 1914-18.*
(Macmillan, New York, 1965).
Illustrated overview.

Totland, John. *No Man's Land: 1918 – The Last Year of the Great War.*
(Doubleday & Co., Garden City, NY, 1980).

Tuchman, Barbara. *The Guns of August.*
(Bantam Books, New York, 1976).
The outbreak and early battles of the war, before the U.S. got involved.

Williams, T. Harry. *The History of American Wars from 1745 to 1918.*
(Alfred A. Knopf, New York, 1981).

Index

Page numbers in *Italics* refer
to illustration